Fred DeRuvo

http://studygrowknow.com

Copyright © 2012 by Study-Grow-Know

All rights reserved. Written permission must be secured from the publisher to use or reproduce any part of this book, except brief quotations in critical reviews or articles.

Published in Scotts Valley, California, by Study-Grow-Know
www.studygrowknow.com • www.adroitpublications.com

Scripture quotations unless otherwise noted, are from The Holy Bible, King James Version. This version is in the public domain.

Images used in this publication (unless otherwise noted) are from clipartconnection.com and used with permission, ©2007 JUPITERIMAGES, and its licensors. All rights reserved.

Any Woodcuts used herein are in the Public Domain and free of copyright.

All Figure illustrations used in this book were created by the author and protected under copyright laws, © 2012, unless otherwise noted.

Cover Design and Interior Layout: Fred DeRuvo

Cover Photos: © mipan - Fotolia.com and © Teemu Lankila - Fotolia.com

Editor: Hannah Richards

Library of Congress Cataloging-in-Publication Data

DeRuvo, Fred, 1957 –

ISBN 0983700680
EAN-13 978-0-9837006-8-5

1. Religion / Biblical Studies / General

CONTENTS

Foreword:		5
Chapter 1:	Seeking God's Face	7
Chapter 2:	Not Mine, But Thine	14
Chapter 3:	Being Sober in Prayer	24
Chapter 4:	Daniel's Battle in Prayer	33
Chapter 5:	King Hezekiah	44
Chapter 6:	Anguish in Gethsemane	52
Chapter 7:	Paul's Prayers	59
Chapter 8:	James Weighs In	64
Chapter 9:	Jude Speaks; Jesus Prays	67
Chapter 10:	Why and When Should We Pray?	74
Chapter 11:	How Should We Pray?	79
Chapter 12:	For What Should We Pray?	82
Chapter 13:	For Whom Should We Pray?	99
Chapter 14:	Give It Up	103
Chapter 15:	The End	106

Praying always with all prayer and supplication in the Spirit, and watching thereunto with all perseverance and supplication for all saints.

– Ephesians 6:18 (KJV)

FOREWORD

I admit I have been doing it incorrectly. I thought that I was correct, but I realize now I wasn't.

Prayer is something that everyone *uses* at one time or another. That's the problem. We normally *use* it to get what we need or in the hopes of getting what we *think* we need.

This book is a work in progress even though it's complete in page count. As an authentic Christian, I will always be learning about prayer. It is something that I cannot avoid.

Prayer in its most raw form is simply talking *with* (not *at*) God. It is communing with Him. It is spending time seeking His will.

All too often, prayer is simply another tool in the Christian's arsenal that he/she pulls out from time to time in order to gain something. We hate to admit that too often we look at God as our personal genie instead of the owner of our souls.

We have to *change* things. We have to stop seeing God in such a disdainful way. It lowers Him. It brings Him down to our level. It reduces His magnificence into something that is far more ordinary and even pedestrian.

God is *not* our genie. He is not there waiting for us to come to Him in order that we might give Him our laundry list of *wants*. Yes, there are numerous places in Scripture that tell us to go boldly before God's throne, making our requests known to Him. We will take some time to look at those to see what they actually say.

I have not "arrived" regarding prayer. I believe that while the Holy Spirit has given me insight into understanding prayer, I have a long way to go before I have learned what God would have me learn to become a better prayer warrior. What I have learned at this point is that while prayer gives me a direct connection to God's ear, as it were, prayer itself is something far more holy, far more beneficent, and far better than I have given it credit for being.

I hope you gain something from this book. It is written in the hopes of helping all of us understand what prayer is and its ultimate purpose.

Fred DeRuvo, March, 2012

Chapter 1
Seeking God's Face

I have long given thought to the area of prayer. The Bible, of course, is filled with examples of prayers that people like King David and many others have prayed. When we think of prayers, we most likely think of the Psalms, or possibly the Lord's own prayer that He taught His disciples with, or His High Priestly prayer recorded in John 17.

Prayer is our lifeline to God. It is entering into conversation with Him. But it is more than that. When I enter into prayer, the first question I ask myself is, *what am I going to pray about?*

There are so many ways to pray, from simple repetition (which God tends to ignore), to heartfelt pleas for God to answer our requests, to taking the time to praise Him for the fact that He exists.

As I look over my own lifetime, I see there have been many types of prayers to God. Many of them, I realize now, were completely selfish. Self was at the center of some of my prayers and Self wanted what it wanted, even providing me with a religious-sounding excuse regarding why I should pray what I prayed.

The truth of the matter is that prayer should be *mainly* one thing. It should be entering into a dialogue with God in order to ascertain *His* will for our lives.

When Jesus told His disciples how to pray, He unfolded something before them that should have impacted the way they approached God. Let's take a few moments to look at that prayer, notably called "The Lord's Prayer," from Matthew 6:9-13.

> *Our Father which art in heaven, Hallowed be thy name.*
> *Thy kingdom come, Thy will be done in earth, as it is in heaven.*
> *Give us this day our daily bread.*
> *And forgive us our debts, as we forgive our debtors.*
> *And lead us not into temptation, but deliver us from evil: For thine is the kingdom, and the power, and the glory, for ever. Amen.*

We note that before Jesus does anything, He praises the Father's Name. The word "hallowed" literally means "*to make holy or sacred, to sanctify or consecrate, to venerate.*"[1] If we ask ourselves whether or not this part of His prayer has been answered, we would have to say that it has not, but we also know that one day it will be answered fully. At some point in the future, every knee will bow before the Lord and all will acknowledge His Lordship and Sovereignty over all things (cf. Romans 14:11).

---

[1] http://en.wikipedia.org/wiki/Hallow (February 1, 2012)

Notice also that Jesus asks the Father to send His Kingdom and to have His will done on earth just as it is perfectly accomplished in heaven. While God has designed the things that occur on this planet to bring us toward the day of absolute fulfillment of His will, the perfection of His will is not being universally and voluntarily practiced yet. There will come a day when the only things that take place in each person's heart, mind and life will perfectly coincide with the will of the Father. We are not there yet.

From there, Jesus moves onto His first temporal request, teaching the people listening that the only thing they should be concerned about is today. "Give us this day our daily bread." Jesus is teaching that we should not waste time worrying about tomorrow, next month, or next year. It is enough to simply be concerned with what is happening during this current 24-hour period in which we are now living.

This, of course, does not mean that we cannot be looking down the road, asking the Lord to make our paths straight and His will obvious for us. It means that with respect to my needs now, I should only be concerned with those needs as they relate to this particular day. I can deal with tomorrow's needs tomorrow.

It is a lesson in walking through this life one day at a time. It is the path that Jesus walked, in which He lived in the moment, not in the future or in the past.

What makes someone a great actor is their ability to actually live in the moment whether they are on the stage or in a movie. Their performance is considered to be real and we are drawn into the play or movie because of that reality they have created. That reality comes from the fact that regardless of how much they have rehearsed, the moment the curtain goes up or the director says "action!" they are in that moment as if it is happening for the very first time.

This is what separates great actors from mediocre actors. Some actors are almost born into it, coming to the craft of acting with the embodiment of reality that makes them stand head and shoulders above others. Other actors can come to that through years of learning and practice.

I recall acting in one play in which I portrayed a bit of a mean land developer who really did not care how much his schemes negatively impacted the people in the town. At one point, I had to give a bit of a threatening speech to another character in the play who was trying to keep me from moving ahead with my plans. I recall that as I began my lines, I started almost slightly trembling inside, not out of fear, but out of intensity. That intensity welled up inside me and came out in a steely tone that surprised even me.

As I finished my line and was just turning to walk off stage, someone in the audience said under their breath, "Oh, tough guy, huh?!" It jolted me slightly because I had been in the moment, and hearing someone from the audience made me realize that I was simply acting the part. Apparently, it had been convincing enough.

Jesus is saying that our life encompasses today and all the moments that comprise today. Do we really know if we will be here tomorrow or even an hour from now? No, we aren't privy to that information, so the best we can do is live our life as if this particular day was our last. In doing so, we will shrug off the things that are unimportant and focus on those things that are important.

Jesus then tells us that we should always harbor an attitude of forgiveness, never one of *unforgiveness*. We should always be quick to forgive because our Father in heaven is quick to forgive us. How can we rightly hold a grudge against someone else when the God of the universe is unwilling to hold a grudge against us? When we sin, we need to confess those sins and He is faithful and just and will forgive them (cf. 1 John 1:9). We should do this same thing with respect to others. We will be treated wrongly in this life. Do we harbor grudges or are we quick to let them go?

Jesus teaches the crowds that God is not One to lead people into or even allow people in the arena of temptation. In other words, what Jesus is saying here is that God prefers to help us *avoid* temptation. Sometimes, though, we wind up tempting ourselves by placing ourselves in a position that encourages us to sin. Jesus is saying that we should count on the Lord to help us avoid those instances when it becomes easy to sin. He will provide the strength if we ask Him.

It is imperative that we have God's armor on every day. It starts with reading His Word and prayer. I'm convinced that what we term as bad things occurring in our lives are messages from God; messages that tell us to seek His face. He isn't trying to trip us up. He isn't trying to make us miserable. He wants our attention, and I believe that as we draw near to Him, we will recognize the strength He provides to overcome all obstacles...*emotionally*. If we cannot be defeated through our emotions, we cannot be defeated.

For those times when evil is a problem, God will also faithfully deliver us from those trials. Now, this does not always mean that He will remove them. It may mean that He will simply uphold us or provide the strength and discernment for us to find our way out through the power of the indwelling Spirit.

Jesus ends with the declaration that everything is God's. Everything belongs to Him, and when all is said and done, the only thing that will exist is God and His Kingdom. God will be glorified in everything.

There are many who ask how a loving God could allow evil. They wonder how a so-called righteous God could stand by when evil obviously parades through this life in many forms.

Well, the truth of the matter is that God gave Adam and Eve free will and it was used to rebel against Him. Sure, God could have stopped that from happening, but then He would have been interfering with free will. Since the time of the fall, God has continued to direct the affairs of this world to their preordained conclusion without impacting our free will (such as it is now).

God did not create automatons. He created individuals with the ability to choose, and it certainly seems to be the case that all those who had absolute free will (with the exception of Jesus) – Satan, Adam and Eve – turned against God. Now, since we came ultimately from Adam and Eve, whose wills had already been turned against God, how can we fare any better? We can't because of the corruption that was passed down to us.

If in our prayer time, we spend most of it asking God to fulfill our requests, I wonder if we are missing the boat. If all we are doing is going before the Lord to bring our requests before Him, then maybe we should look again at the reason we are going before the throne in the first place.

God is certainly there to help us. He wants us to bring our requests to Him, but He also wants a good deal more. He wants our lives, our attitudes, and our commitment to Him to be that we want Him to live His life in and through us as much as He wants that to happen.

Colossians 4:2-3 says, *"Continue in prayer, and watch in the same with thanksgiving; 3Withal praying also for us, that God would open unto us a door of utterance, to speak the mystery of Christ, for which I am also in bonds."*

Note that Paul's main concern for himself is that he would have doors open to preach the gospel. We need to compare our requests to those of the apostle. We will talk more about the apostle Paul later on in this book.

As I look back through the corridor of time regarding all the requests I've brought to God, I am left to wonder if I have not been guilty of two things: 1) using God for my genie, and 2) not believing that He had/has an actual plan for my life.

It seems clear enough from the life of Jesus that He did not worry. He didn't hurry either. He spent a good deal of time with the Father in prayer, and in fact, it seems that whenever He had an extra moment or two during His public ministry He could be found praying to the Father. All of this should be an example to us regarding how we are to pray and what we should expect from prayer.

Can you imagine if every time you spoke to your spouse, you simply went into their presence and began asking them for things? You never really talked with them, but simply asked things of them. What kind of relationship would you wind up having with that person over time? It would be extremely one-sided, wouldn't it?

Do you want to actually *know* the Lord more each day, or are you content with simply asking Him to do things for you, many times under the guise that by doing those things for you He's really accomplishing His will for your life?

There is a great deal to prayer, and I have certainly not arrived to the place where I believe I am done learning. My wife and I recently celebrated our 25th wedding anniversary. It seems like yesterday, in many ways. I love my wife and I can honestly say that as much as I feel I know her, as I look back over the past twenty-five years it is clear how much more I have come to know her because of that time spent together. I'm certainly not done getting to know her, and though we will come to know each other better as time progresses, we will never come to the end of knowing each other. I will never be able to say, "*Well, I guess there is nothing else I need to know about you,*" to my wife.

If people are this deep and multi-faceted, how much *more* so is God?

Chapter 2
Not Mine, But Thine ...

I have been trying to honestly assess my prayer life and have come to some conclusions. When I pray, I often bring my list of requests, but I realize that I rarely end my prayers with the statement that Jesus made in the Garden of Gethsemane noted in the title of this chapter. Why is that?

I believe it is for a couple of reasons:

- Selfishness
- Little attempt to discern His actual will

That may seem obvious, but I challenge you to be mindful of these two indicators the next time you seek the Lord in prayer. In fact, when you go into your prayer closet, determine first why you are there. Are you there to ask God to do something for you? Are you there to present a request that for some reason you think He may not be aware of, or are you there to worship Him first, determine His will second, and praise Him for His provision third?

As I mentioned previously, often my prayers can seem to me to be simply matters of a perfunctory nature. I have "needs," and I take them to Him. I also mentioned that sometimes – maybe more often than not – I go to Him with my own preconceived ideas of how I expect God to answer and respond to my requests.

I recall one instance way back in Bible College, probably thirty or so years ago. I had just begun my very first term at Philadelphia College of Bible and I had a special grant from the government that allowed me to pay for my tuition and my books. The trouble was – as I found out after purchasing some books – that I was supposed to buy all of my books at the same time so that there would be one total purchase per semester. I didn't know that, and when I went back to buy the rest of my books, I was told that I would have to pay cash for them since I had already purchased books against my account previously.

Well, as you can imagine, I was nervous. I thought, *"What am I going to do now?"* I left the bookstore and, after making a quick trip to accounting, headed up to my room, where I literally got on my knees and asked God to provide a way. As I prayed, I began to release the frustration and tension that had been caused by this new situation. In fact, I specifically recall saying to the Lord something along the lines of, *"Lord, I really need to be able to purchase those additional books for my classes, but I do not have the money for it. If you could open the door for that to happen, I would really appreciate it."* As I continued to pray, I experienced a change of outlook. I then prayed, *"Lord, if you do not want me to buy these additional books now, then that's fine. I will use the books from the library to complete my studies until I can earn money from my job to purchase my own books."*

It was actually a very liberating situation. I knew what I wanted as I went into prayer, but on this particular occasion I agreed with the Lord that maybe He did not want to provide the additional money at this point. If so, then I also knew He would provide a way for me to be able to use the necessary books for my classes. In either case, the way the Lord answered the prayer was completely up to Him.

Feeling completely at peace about the situation, I went down to accounting, where the folks in the bookstore had told me I should go to double-check with them. I had been there earlier and they had told me to come back later that day after they had time to check things out.

I arrived at accounting and stood in line about ten people back from the front. As I moved closer, the lady behind the counter saw me, smiled and said, "*You're fine. You can go purchase your books*" and gave me the necessary voucher for the bookstore. As you can imagine, I was elated, but up until that point I was not aware of how the Lord would respond. I really would have been fine either way, but of course this way was by far easier.

As I look over my life since that point, I realize that on too many occasions I never give the Lord an option to respond to my prayers His way. I go before Him, lay out my requests, and then leave, hoping (not necessarily expecting) He will answer me according to my wishes.

Can you imagine a slave going to the master and asking the master to do things his (the slave's) way? That would be absurd! Normally, a slave in Roman times would go to the master with the need and simply wait for the master to respond. The master would tell the slave how he (the slave) should do something or what he (the master) was going to do about the need. As Christians, do we do this with God, or do we simply go to Him with our requests and give Him little to no room to decide how He wants to respond?

I recall many occasions where I left my prayer time not sure of what God would do but really wanting Him to do it my way. How is that allowing God to be God? How is that making Him Lord of my life? It's not, plain and simple.

If I am not willing to do what Jesus did as He suffered emotionally and prayed in the Garden of Gethsemane, then I don't think I have any business going to the Lord in the first place! I note that once Jesus finally released the entire upcoming (and horrendous) situation to the Father, He was at peace.

Please note that in Luke's account of the situation in the Garden of Gethsemane, Jesus was emotionally racked with pain, so much so that He began sweating drops of blood. As He prayed that the upcoming "cup" would be removed from Him, Jesus always finished with the words, "*My Father, if this cannot pass away unless I drink it, Your will be done*" (Matthew 26:42b).

If Jesus did that, how much more should we do that with every request we bring to the Father? We have no excuse, yet I have spent a good portion of my own prayer life dictating to God – yes, dictating – that He would do it my way. How tragic and sinful is that?

It is obviously fine to present our wants to God. Jesus did this in Gethsemane. However, if we do not end it (and mean it) with "not mine, but your will be done," then I believe we are opening ourselves up to confusion, frustration, and possibly even sinful reactions to His will because we are only prepared for His response if it coincides with our will.

I notice that after Jesus won this battle through prayer, He was ready to move forward. He came to the point of letting go of His own wants in favor of the Father's, and because of that, He came to terms with it and peace enveloped Him. *"Behold, the hour is at hand and the Son of Man is being betrayed into the hands of sinners. Get up, let us be going; behold, the one who betrays Me is at hand!"* (Matthew 26:45b-46)

Here we note that Jesus is fully in command. He is in charge, allowing Himself to be arrested illegally and illegally tried by godless men. Can you imagine standing as judge of the God of the universe?! This is what Jesus allowed because He knew it was the Father's will – and thank God for it, because without it we would have no chance to receive salvation; it would not exist to be offered to us.

As I look back over my life and all of my prayers, I realize that too often, I have not given God any room to act according to His will. Because of this, I have experienced frustration (I was expecting a specific answer according to the way I had prayed) because the answer did not arrive as I expected it to arrive. This frustration created an attitude of sinfulness, and I regret that tremendously. However, God is so patient that He allowed those things to occur so that I would learn how He wanted me to pray.

If I look at the Psalms, I don't see the type of requests and minutiae from David that often is included in my prayers. I see a large picture in the prayers from the mouth of David. Yes, there were times when he was greatly concerned for his own life, but even there, he normally ends his prayer with praise to the Lord.

Whose life is it, anyway? If – as I stated earlier – I am a citizen of heaven because through salvation I have been transferred out of the kingdom of darkness into the Kingdom of Light, then where does my allegiance lie? Whom do I serve, my SELF, or God? Obviously, it cannot be both.

More than anything, I want to pray for His will and His alone. I fully believe that the more I see and comprehend that my citizenship is actually not on this planet, the easier it will be to let go of the things that tend to bind me to this earth.

The world is speeding toward the apocalypse, and too many Christians are praying only about their own concerns. We are too busy worrying about how the Lord is going to do this or that, and hopefully, He will do it according to the way we pray. We are way too concerned about having far more than we need, and we believe the additional is also what we "need."

I want to be a man after God's own heart. I want to end each prayer (and mean it) with "not my will, but yours be done." I want Him to show me where He is leading me, not where I am trying to lead Him. How can I call Him Lord and have it any other way? Didn't Jesus say that very same thing? "*Why do you call Me, 'Lord, Lord,' and do not do what I say?*" (Luke 6:46) Excellent question, isn't it?

If God has given us things to do, then shouldn't we be spending more time in prayer asking Him to make His path clear? I have noted all the times I literally begged God to do something according to my will only to end up thoroughly frustrated. I was looking for the wrong thing and it was never coming.

A few years ago, my sister went to be with the Lord. She is home. She is happy. She is healthy, and most importantly, she is worshiping Jesus face to face! Is there anything better than that?

During the week just prior to her death, she was in the hospital in a coma. You can imagine how I prayed. I ceaselessly asked God to restore her to health. All day long and into the night, I reminded Him of my request. This went on for three days.

Finally, on the fourth day, I wanted to begin again asking Him to restore my sister to health, but the words would simply not come. Oh, I could have said them, but they would have meant absolutely nothing. The Lord graciously and patiently let me storm the gates of heaven with my selfish (yet understandable) request to raise my sister to health. Finally, He broke through, and the sense I got was that it was simply not His will. That was final. He was not angry that I had prayed the way I did, but not once had I prayed for His will to be done where my sister was concerned. Not once.

Finally, I just simply stopped. Then I said, "*Lord, you know all things. You not only know what is best for my sister, but your will has been predetermined here. If it is such that you will be taking my sister home, then so be it, Lord. Your will is perfect and reigns supreme. I thank you for it.*"

As you might imagine, that was a very difficult prayer to pray because it meant that I was acknowledging my sister was going to die and I would not see her again until I died. However, I felt that it was okay to continue to pray, and as I did, I asked the Lord to grant one request – if it was His will. My one request was that my sister would open her eyes and we could "connect" so that I could say good-bye. Ever since she entered the hospital (before I arrived) she had been in a coma. I found out later that she had flatlined twice with the paramedics before they were able to get her to the hospital.

That day I went to the hospital, and after lunch my brother-in-law, nephew and I stood in my sister's hospital room. There she was, the same as always, machines doing her breathing and no real brain activity. The nurse was also there, and as I watched she lifted up each of my sister's eyelids and shone a flashlight into her eyes, which were looking straight down into the bottom of her lids. Her pupil did not dilate and there was no movement at all. I asked what that meant – duh! – and the nurse told me there was no brain activity.

She left and we prayed. As we prayed, I glanced up and gently lifted one of my sister's eyelids. She was actually looking right at me! I released it and then continued praying. I looked up again, and this time both of her eyelids were fluttering and then they both opened...wide. She stared directly at me! I knew that we had made contact.

Later that evening, we received a call from the hospital and we were told "something had changed." When we arrived, my sister had gone onto glory where she blissfully lives now. I still cried like a baby, but God was so gracious in answering my prayer – a prayer He did not have to answer.

I am endeavoring to pray only for His will. I have a lot of requests, requests that often seem to go ignored. I think it's largely because, as James says, I have been asking amiss. *"You ask and do not receive, because you ask with wrong motives, so that you may spend it on your pleasures"* (James 4:3). Yep, that's me, constantly asking with the wrong motives. How about you? Can you say with surety that every time you go before the Lord's throne, you are free of ulterior motives?

If we are truly Jesus' slaves (and is there a better Master?) and if we are truly citizens of heaven, then how can we live as if we are in charge of our own lives, as if we know better than God? Is He working in and through us to accomplish His will, or are we working to accomplish what we believe is His will?

It is time for authentic Christians to realize that not only is our time short on this earth, but much of what we do will not matter when we compare it with eternity. The number of books I've sold won't matter. The amount of money I may have spent to "get my books out there" will not matter. The only thing that matters is whether or not I have been fulfilling God's will or mine.

Paul brings this into sharp focus for us in a letter he wrote to the Corinthians: *"For no man can lay a foundation other than the one which is laid, which is Jesus Christ.* ***Now if any man builds on the foundation*** *with gold, silver, precious stones,* ***wood, hay, straw****, each man's* *work will become evident; for the day will show it because it is to be revealed with fire, and the fire itself will test the quality of each man's work. If any man's work which he has built on it remains, he will receive a reward. If any man's work is burned up, he will suffer loss; but he himself will be saved, yet so as through fire"* (1 Corinthians 3:11-15).

Paul cannot be speaking of non-Christians here because of the phrase I have bolded. A non-Christian builds his house on the sand and is not saved. Paul is speaking of Christians here – authentic Christians. He is referencing the time when we will all stand before Jesus in judgment: judgment not for salvation, but for rewards. Everything I have done, everything I have said and everything I have thought will go through the fires of judgment. The things that remain will provide me with a reward. Those things that do not remain but are burned up will give me no reward. In the end, a Christian could have all his works burned up and he will still have his salvation, because it will not burn up.

This is a very sobering principle here. We shouldn't do these things because we want rewards. We should do them because we want to glorify Him. Any crowns of rewards we get will be fittingly and reverently tossed at His feet anyway, according to Revelation. Why? It is because without His presence and strength in our lives, those rewards would not be possible. In essence, then, Jesus grants salvation and enables us to live lives that glorify Him. In the process, we receive rewards that He enables and helps us to earn through the works we do: works done in His strength, not our own.

I am endeavoring to revamp my prayer life so that I only ask for those things that are His will. When I do not know His will, then I am required to leave it completely up to Him. Even when I do know His will, I still need to leave it up to Him.

Jesus is our rock and our salvation. He is our Master and provider. He has stated He will never leave or forsake us (Hebrews 13:5). If that is the truth – and it is – how is it I can doubt that He will provide for my needs? I truly must have the same attitude that Jesus had, *"who, although He existed in the form of God, did not regard equality with God a thing to be grasped, but emptied Himself, taking the form of a bond-servant, and being made in the likeness of men. Being found in appearance as a man, He humbled Himself by becoming obedient to the point of death, even death on a cross. For this reason also, God highly exalted Him, and bestowed on Him the name which is above every name, so that at the name of Jesus EVERY KNEE WILL BOW, of those who are in heaven and on earth and under the earth, and that every tongue will confess that Jesus Christ is Lord, to the glory of God the Father"* (Philippians 2:6-11).

If Jesus Himself did that, how can I *not*?

Chapter 3
Being Sober in Prayer

As noted, prayer is talking with God. However, it is far more than that. It is because we are Christians that we are in the midst of constant spiritual struggle. The prayer offered in faith is likely one of the best weapons we have against the wiles of the enemy with respect to that specific *spiritual battle*. We do not see the spiritual battle that continually rages all around us. However, we are involved in it whether we like it or not.

Because of the spiritual nature of the battle, the battlefront is wherever we are *physically*. That place should always be the point of entry to our awareness of the war that continues. We must remind ourselves to actively engage the enemy, and that is only done through prayer. In prayer, we should quote God's holy and powerful Word. We should not be afraid to use His Word as the true sword of the Spirit that it is. As the warrior on the battlefield chooses the best weapon and learns how to wield it, so too must the Christian understand the true essence of prayer in order to defeat the enemy.

The devil, we are told by Peter, constantly wages war against the saints. He never sleeps, never takes time out to rest, and is always on the prowl to bring down God's children. Peter tells us, "*Humble yourselves therefore under the mighty hand of God, that he may exalt you in due time: Casting all your care upon him; for he careth for you.* ***Be sober, be vigilant; because your adversary the devil, as a roaring lion, walketh about, seeking whom he may devour****: Whom resist stedfast in the faith, knowing that the same afflictions are accomplished in your brethren that are in the world*" (1 Peter 5:6-9; emphasis added).

Notice that the admonition by Peter is first of all to be sober, or sober-minded. Any soldier who has ever fought in any battle will tell you that one of the keys to survival is being *alert*. Being alert must not come and go. It must be constant because it is above all things the first prerequisite for survival.

A soldier who lets his guard down, loses sight of his surroundings, or takes his situation for granted will soon fall to the enemy. Being alert is sacrosanct for remaining alive.

I have served as a voluntary chaplain in a local jail. When I would go into the "tank" (jail vernacular for the areas of cells where inmates are kept), I was always alert. After a time of getting to know some of the inmates, it is easy to let your guard down. You cannot do this. One quickly realizes that these inmates are people who have done, in some cases, very bad things, but they are still people. They need God just as much as the agnostic or atheist who appears to us to be a moral person.

The trouble is that over time it is easy to simply see them as people, not realizing that they are behind bars for a reason. They often become very adept at manipulation, and one of the key things that are drummed into all volunteer chaplains is that when any requests are personally made of you, the response is, "write a kite." A "kite" is simply a note that is directed to the head chaplain. Everything must go through the head chaplain, as it is his responsibility to respond to the inmate's request. It is not mine.

If I allow myself to lose sight of my goal – which is to visit the jail for the sole purpose of ministering to the inmates through Bible study and prayer – I may become inadvertently caught up in something that I will regret later, even if it is not illegal. People are people and we all have habits that should be broken. Inmates are no different, except that their habits may be tougher to break. Many are in jail due to serious drug addictions or gang problems. These men, while wanting to change their lives, may not have an easy time doing so and want to draw you into their personal lives so that they can begin to rely on you once they transfer to another jail or when they become paroled. This must be avoided, and what can make this difficult is the fact that many of these inmates have no one else they can turn to, so they turn to you.

Many of these situations are extremely innocuous. Some start out innocuously but can lead to something more. In all cases, alertness must be maintained so that chaplains are not caught up into something that could harm them or the inmate.

Being alert is the primary attitude that a chaplain must wear at all times when in the jail environment. Every Christian must wear that same attitude at all times. We cannot allow our demeanor to relax because our enemy never relaxes. He never takes a time out, nor does he ever sleep or need to eat or simply grow tired from the daily workload. Satan has many advantages over us including his awesome power that he is allowed to wield against God's children, as God allows. His goal is to wear us down to make it easier for us to fall into sin.

Peter understood from personal experience how important it was and is to always be aware of the fact that Satan has one primary purpose, and that is to defeat God's elect. Paul essentially states this same thing when he points out that he (Paul) is not unaware of the schemes of the enemy (cf. 2 Corinthians 2:11). In the verse in 2 Corinthians, Paul simply states, *"for we are not ignorant of his devices."*

What soldier would go out onto the battle field completely unaware of his opponent's strategies? The only time that might happen is when an opposing army does a sneak attack in which there has been no time to prepare for the onslaught.

We can also apply this truth to the alertness of arena sporting events. Prior to big games, teams will often watch the game videos that highlight the team they are going up against in a big match. The reason for this is simple. It allows the players who will be opposing that team to learn or refresh their memories regarding how that team plays. They may also learn about any weak spots the opposing team may have and how often they might use the same type of play repeatedly. This is obviously done to give the team a leg up on the opposition.

For these players, watching team videos of actual games and then going out to play that opposing team while forgetting everything they just viewed would result in a big loss. Teams watch the videos for the purpose of learning how to overcome the opposing team, not to lose.

Prayer allows us to become and remain alert. Prayer keeps us on our toes, as it were, constantly waiting for God to move and show us what we should be doing. Prayer appropriates not only knowledge of God's will but the strength to complete His will. Prayer also brings us directly into the Lord's presence and shines the light on areas in our life that fall short.

Just like the football player who realizes that his opponent has some moves that will beat him if he is not careful, prayer brings to light the areas of weakness that we must consider. The football player who sees his own potential areas of weakness does not become depressed. He sees these as potential areas for growth. He sees and understands what he is doing wrong and how to correct the problem areas. It is nothing personal, and because of that he does not fall into depression. It is very pragmatic for the football player or athlete. It is a necessary part of the training process.

It is through prayer that we first see areas of weakness and defect. These areas are brought to our attention through the loving guidance of the indwelling Holy Spirit. These areas may be sin, or they simply may be areas of spiritual immaturity in which the Spirit desires our cooperation so that they can be fixed. Once we see these faults, we can willingly confess any and all sin that may be associated with them in our life that the Holy Spirit brings to our mind. Once our sins are confessed, we can come to a point of submission to God for His purposes in and through us.

Prayer helps us to distinguish between what is *worthy* and what is *unworthy*. Prayer, coupled with faith and knowledge of God's Word, presents an insurmountable source of weaponry against our foe, the devil. Prayer is the very thing that keeps us from stumbling co-actively with Christ's strength in and through us. It is through prayer that we learn to resist Satan.

Prayer is probably the most worthy pursuit that any Christian can endeavor to undertake. Let's be cautious here, though. Prayer is *not* the Christian presenting his or her giant wish list to God. It is not me desiring to use God as my personal genie. It is not the Christian trying to convince God that if He would only provide a better car, a better job, or a better whatever, then he or she would be able to serve Him more faithfully.

Prayer is first and foremost *submission to* God, not *demanding from* God! We see a number of individuals throughout the Bible who were victorious in prayer, and they were victorious for a very important reason. We hear of victorious prayer and victorious Christian living today, but much of it bears little resemblance to the truth of God's Word and Christ's life. Much of it is nothing more than seeing God as the great Genie in the Sky who is there to serve me and my purposes. Not only is this far from the truth, but it is blasphemy in its purest form. We are not here on this planet to serve ourselves or to somehow make God into our Wish Giver. We are on this planet to serve the Living God and to bring glory to Him. This can only occur when we are *willing* to be made willing to serve Him by turning over every area of our life to Him and His purposes. He has *not* promised us our best life now. It is truly that simple in theory. It is where the rubber meets the road for the Christian in this life. How well we submit to Him is directly tied to the type of prayer we live.

David was a man who loved God – was a man after God's own heart – and searched diligently for Him. He is known as the author of most of the Psalms and the first king after King Saul to follow God with all of his heart. In spite of his failures, God remained with him because David turned back to God in true repentance. Even after his terrible sins of adultery and murdering Uriah, Bathsheba's husband, he *returned* to God in full repentance. He recommitted himself to following God. Yet, his sins had consequences that God allowed to occur. First, the baby that Bathsheba carried died after birth. Next, the sword became part of the house of David. His own sons turned against him in anger.

None of this set well with David, but he created his own problems by focusing on what he should not have been focusing on. Nonetheless, God forgave when David returned.

Jesus, as God *and* Man, bridged the gap between the two testaments. He was also a Man of prayer, constantly submitting Himself to the Father as an example that we should follow. You cannot look seriously at prayer without looking at the God-Man who lived His entire life by prayer.

Paul was a man of the New Covenant, the covenant that came into being when Jesus died and rose again, shedding His blood for the remission of sins. Paul was among the first fruits of this new covenant, and Jesus Himself specifically handpicked him for a special purpose as he traveled along with road to Damascus for the purposes of arresting those Jews who had converted to Christianity. Paul understood the *meaning* of prayer, the *benefits* of prayer, and the *reason* why we should never give up on prayer.

These men knew what it meant to battle in the spiritual realm through prayer. They were not novices. They learned a great deal through the act of prayer. Remember, this is not prayer for prayer's sake. It is prayer *with a purpose.* That purpose is to determine God's will. As a byproduct of prayer, we also learn what it is that we want and whether or not our wants fall in line with God's wants as He seeks to work in and through us for His good pleasure.

As stated, Satan wants to wear us down. He will do whatever it takes to bring us to sin. He does so by attacking us in this physical realm in many ways. It is obvious that Satan is a being that essentially inhabits the spiritual realm but certainly has access to us in this realm. We know that from the book of Job. We are not immune from his attacks, and Peter notes that Satan is like a roaring lion. One of the things he loves best is to roam around just looking for victims, Christians he can *devour*.

The other day I was watching a history special on Vietnam. It was a very interesting documentary with a good deal of eyewitness accounts from the soldiers who were there and fought the enemy. At one point, the soldiers had worked their way north through South Vietnam toward the demilitarized zone (DMZ). It was just shy of the DMZ that they came across a village.

The village itself was in South Vietnam, so the soldiers knew that they had to defend that village from the onslaught of the Vietcong. The problem was that there is virtually no difference between people of South Vietnam and North Vietnam. If you remove the military clothing and put on regular clothes that people wore in Vietnam, how would you know who the enemy was by simply looking at them?

One particular soldier indicated that as he was moving through the jungle not far from the village, he felt something or someone behind him. He glanced to his left and saw a shadow out of the corner of his eye. He turned to see an elderly Vietnamese woman behind him, pointing a loaded small crossbow at him. Her finger was on the trigger. She was obviously trying to sneak up on him to get in a well-placed shot that she hoped would kill him.

The soldier simply went into automatic mode and without thinking about it, lifted his rifle and shot the woman before she had time to do anything. She died right on that spot. Had the soldier seen this woman in the village, he would not have thought, "*Hmmm, there is an enemy. I'd better keep my eye on her!*" because she blended in with the other people who were part of the village already.

This is the way it is in the spiritual realm. We cannot see our enemy, and because of that, he has the upper hand. This is exactly why we are told that we do not battle flesh and blood but powers and principalities over spiritual realms (cf. Ephesians 6:12). Our battle is not against other human beings, even though it may seem like it or appear to be the case. Our battle is in the heavenly realms, where Satan is still allowed to reign, controlling his troops of demons so that his will is accomplished. All of this takes place, of course, under God's watchful eyes.

We cannot see our enemy, but through God's Word we learn how he works. Knowing how he works and knowing the power we have in Christ to overcome through prayer is something that is too important not to know. It can mean the difference between growing in Christ or falling backwards. The former takes work. The latter requires us to do nothing. Too many seem to be doing just that.

Chapter 4
Daniel's Battle in Prayer

Daniel was not only a man of *prayer* but a man of *habit*. As we read about his life, it seems clear that he was also a man with tremendous *patience* and *calm*. He never seemed to be in any kind of a hurry. He was never at odds with himself or God. He never seemed to be concerned for his own life, nor did he ever seem to doubt God.

In these ways, Daniel is nearly a perfect picture of Jesus Christ. Jesus, as we will see, was completely in tune with the Father's will. He never rushed to get anywhere, even after his friend Lazarus died. Jesus took the time to stop and talk to people, giving them His time because of *their* need.

Jesus learned early what it meant to die to self and seek only the Father's will. Because of these things, Jesus' life was the picture of serenity even when it was difficult.

So it was with Daniel, who also seemed completely unflappable. It did not matter what human being was seemingly in control of the physical kingdoms where Daniel lived. It did not matter what new laws were passed. It did not matter to Daniel who worked behind the scenes to attempt to have him killed. None of that seemed at all to matter to Daniel. Daniel was *content*, leaning fully on God's mighty arm. I'm sure he experienced tensions within, but the answer was always met through prayer.

Daniel's prayer life was one to which we should all aspire. Not only did Daniel pray daily, but he prayed *three* times daily; opening his windows/shutters that faced Jerusalem and kneeling, he entered the throne room of God. It was there he came spiritually face to face with the God of the universe and his own puny humanity in comparison.

Daniel entreated God often on behalf of his people, the Israelites. Daniel, like Jesus, was literally a stopgap for Israel, like a high priest. Little did the average Jewish person realize just how often Daniel stood in for them time after time. Yet, such was the case.

On one particular occasion, Daniel was in deep prayer and had, in fact, been praying for 21 days before any answer arrived. Finally, Gabriel arrived and even interrupted Daniel as he resolutely continued in prayer, seemingly undaunted by the wait he was experiencing.

Gabriel quickly explained that he had been kept at bay by the Prince of Persia, likely a reference to one of the demonic overlords of that region (Persia:; present-day Iran) who fought against God's angels to keep God's will from occurring.

We see this played out in Daniel 9. Here, during Daniel's prayer for his people – the Jews of Israel – he requests a number of things that I want to look at. In fact, it would help us greatly to take the time to break down Daniel's prayer in order to understand how he prayed and why he prayed as he did. His example is something from which we can learn and which we can apply to our lives.

In chapter 9 of Daniel we are introduced to Darius, and according to Daniel, this is Darius' first year in power. Like numerous prophets of old, Daniel provides this information to us to give us a timeline of history. This allows us to determine what else was happening during that period of time, and important facts such as these also lend greater authenticity to Daniel's book.

After this brief introduction, Daniel explains that he had been searching the Scriptures. In fact, he had been studying the writings of another prophet, Jeremiah, and in doing so had learned that the number of years – seventy – which would complete the current judgment against Israel was nearly complete. As can be expected, he was excited at the prospect that the Jewish people would be released from bondage, so he began to pray – not only to commit the Jewish people to the Lord, but to recognize that they had received from God what they deserved because of their failure to live up to God's standards.

In essence, then, Daniel was praying the prayer of a high priest. Let's take a look at what he says.

Daniel 9:4-6
Alas, O Lord, the great and awesome God, who keeps His covenant and lovingkindness for those who love Him and keep His commandments, we have sinned, committed iniquity, acted wickedly and rebelled, even turning aside from Your commandments and ordinances. Moreover, we have not listened to Your servants the prophets, who spoke in Your name to our kings, our princes, our fathers and all the people of the land.

The first thing Daniel does is to praise God for:

- *Being great*
- *Being awesome*
- *Being consistent*

Daniel calls God great, awesome and a keeper of His covenants to those who keep His commandments. We need to remember that the nation of Israel was charged with keeping the Law. For Israel, this goes way beyond the Ten Commandments that we are familiar with today. For the Jewish person, there were 613 Laws that God gave the nation through Moses. This is why Paul says that those who attempt to live under the law are obligated to keep all of it (cf. Galatians 5:3). When he says that, he is not merely referring to ten of them but *all* 613 of them. This is what the entire book of Galatians is about, but if we focus in on the third chapter of Galatians, we learn that all who live under the law are under a curse.

As authentic Christians, we are required to live God's *moral code*, which is generally found within the Ten Commandments. The first part of the Ten Commandments deal with how we are to relate to God, while the second part of the commandments teach us how to relate to other people. This is God's moral code and it is why the entire law can be summed up in two commands: 1) love the Lord with all your heart, and 2) love your neighbor as yourself (cf. Matthew 22:34-37).

Daniel recognized that those who truly love God will walk in His commandments. Paul clarifies that those who live *under* the umbrella of the Law, thinking it will save them, are simply living under a curse. The curse exists because no one (save Jesus) can live under the Law perfectly, *from the heart*. Jesus made this distinction during His public ministry (cf. Matthew 5-7).

Notice that Daniel then segues into an admission of guilt. He admits that "we" have sinned, and he is including himself in that as he kneels before God, interceding for the nation of Israel.

Daniel has no qualms about recognizing and admitting guilt. He states that the Israelites (of which he is part) have:

- *Committed iniquity (broken God's laws)*
- *Acted wickedly and rebelled (allowed SELF to reign)*
- *Turned from God's commands and ordinances*
- *Ignored the men God had sent to warn the people of Israel*

These are terrible things and we are all guilty of them. The problem with Israel was that, like today, they did not see their error. They didn't see it then, nor do they see it now. They want God's blessing, but they are unwilling to recognize their own failure to heed God's warnings and fulfill His will voluntarily for their lives.

Daniel cuts right to the heart of the matter, acknowledging to God what God already knows. The people were in solid rebellion against God.

Now that the time of release is drawing close, Daniel wants to confess Israel's sins to God in hopes of making amends with Him. Daniel wants God to give them a fresh chance to start over, to make things right, and to prove to the world that Israel can be faithful to God, the Creator of their nation.

From here, Daniel goes right back to recognizing the truth about God and the truth about Israel.

Daniel 9:7-8
Righteousness belongs to You, O Lord, but to us open shame, as it is this day—to the men of Judah, the inhabitants of Jerusalem and all Israel, those who are nearby and those who are far away in all the countries to which You have driven them, because of their un-

faithful deeds which they have committed against You. Open shame belongs to us, O Lord, to our kings, our princes and our fathers, because we have sinned against You.

Daniel has absolutely no interest in whitewashing anything. He tells it as it is, and this is what God wants. God does not simply want to hear these *words*. He wants to see a heart attitude that matches, and He sees this in Daniel. Is it any wonder that Daniel was a man greatly loved by God (cf. Daniel 9:23)?

Daniel understands that what Israel has suffered she has suffered because of the sins of her people. Israel has been completely unfaithful, guilty of worshiping other gods and rebelling against God's love and truth. Israel has been guilty of putting God to the test and stretching His patience to the limit, yet please notice that the first thing Daniel states is that God is righteous in all His dealings with Israel.

Daniel has not once complained about Israel's treatment by the nations and her seeming neglect by God Himself. Daniel sees this as being fully deserved by Israel. It is the natural consequence of failing to love God with all your heart, mind, and soul above all things.

When the Israelites lived in Israel and had a place to worship they had gotten into a rut of going through the motions where God was concerned. Worship meant little to nothing to them. It was simply something they did because it was required. It was the rare Israelite who saw beyond the ritual to actually understand that seen properly, this – for Israel – was the way to establish a walking relationship with God.

This is something we need to ask ourselves about our own life. Do we pray as a matter of formality or because it's expected? Do we go to church because that's what we've done for years and cannot see doing anything else?

Do we do these things, or do we revel in the fact that we are in true relationship with God through Jesus Christ? Is our life a reflection of the way we *feel* toward God, or is it one of ritualized service that bears *no fruit* and directs *no glory to* God?

These are important questions that we must take the time to deal with because the honest answers to these questions will help us understand the quality of our relationship with God. We are *in relationship* with God because of our faith in Jesus. However, has our relationship with God grown over the years? Has our trust in Him increased? Do we feel as though we know Him better today than we did yesterday? Does our relationship with Him bear fruit?

Do we understand that God is changing us into the image of His Son? Are we cooperating with that change or unknowingly working against Him because of the ritualistic nature of our relationship?

Maybe we need to look deeply in the mirror to discern what God sees. Maybe we should take the time out to pray as Daniel did so that our excuses will fall by the wayside and we will simply and readily agree with God that we have rebelled, that we have ignored Him and His moral code, and that we have not listened to the truth of His Word, nor have we taken it to heart.

There is always work that can be done in any relationship, and certainly, our relationship with God is no different. We need to understand that the relationship we have with God is such that He is the Master and we are the slave. Jude says we are "bond-servants." Think about that. A bond-servant is someone who is attached to the master, either directly or emotionally.

During Jesus' day, slaves who learned to appreciate and respect their masters might make the decision to become a lifelong slave by having their ear fitted with a ring. This ring signified that they had voluntarily enslaved themselves to their master for life. To do this, they would be taken to the door and their earlobe would be placed against the frame of the door. An awl would then be used to make a hole in the lobe and a ring would be placed through it. It was painful, but to the slave who had made this decision, it was fully worth it.

That slave was saying to the world that their master was fair. That slave was acknowledging that they had tremendous respect and even love for their master.

Look at one of Abraham's slaves. Abraham sent his trusted slave to find a wife for his son, Isaac. In Genesis 24:12-14 we read the words of the slave as he prayed to God to be merciful to his master, Abraham.

"He said, 'O Lord, the God of my master Abraham, please grant me success today, and show lovingkindness to my master Abraham. Behold, I am standing by the spring, and the daughters of the men of the city are coming out to draw water; now may it be that the girl to whom I say, "Please let down your jar so that I may drink," and who answers, "Drink, and I will water your camels also"—may she be the one whom You have appointed for Your servant Isaac; and by this I will know that You have shown lovingkindness to my master.'"

Notice that several times in the above verses the servant uses the term "master" in referring to Abraham. He is praying on behalf of his master Abraham, and it is clear that this servant loved his master and wanted the Lord to bless Abraham.

This should be our attitude with respect to God. We should want to see the Lord's will done at all costs and above all things. Abraham's servant did not pray for himself specifically, only that he would be successful in fulfilling his mission for Abraham. Earlier, Abraham provided an "out" for the servant if the he did all that he could and was not able to fulfill the mission, but it is obvious that the servant wanted this prayer answered not for himself, but for Abraham.

Daniel is essentially doing the same thing. Yes, he is praying for Israel so that they will turn around and begin to live their lives in such a way that will bring glory to God. The juxtaposition between God and Israel is made obvious when Daniel declares that God is *righteous* but Israel lives in *shame*. He calls it "open shame" because God punished Israel in front of the nations and allowed certain nations to overcome Israel and take them captive.

Because God allowed this, these nations then could easily come to the conclusion that Israel's God is nothing – completely powerless – and that their gods are better. This erroneous thinking is shameful because it is not based on the truth. Israel brought that shame out into the open. This open shame extends all the way to the kings of Israel because of their sin against God.

Daniel 9:9-15
To the Lord our God belong compassion and forgiveness, for we have rebelled against Him; nor have we obeyed the voice of the LORD our God, to walk in His teachings which He set before us through His servants the prophets. Indeed all Israel has transgressed Your law and turned aside, not obeying Your voice; so the curse has been poured out on us, along with the oath which is written in the law of Moses the servant of God, for we have sinned against Him. Thus He has confirmed His words which He had spoken against us and against our rulers who ruled us, to bring on us great calamity; for under the whole heaven there has not been done anything like what was done to Jerusalem. As it is written in the law of Moses, all this calamity has come on us; yet we have not sought the favor of the LORD our God by turning from our iniquity and giving attention to Your truth. Therefore the LORD has kept the calamity in store and brought it on us; for the LORD our God is righteous with respect to all His deeds which He has done, but we have not obeyed His voice.

These verses – nine through fifteen – point out the difference between God and Israel. He is compassionate and forgiving. Israel has rebelled and disobeyed God. Daniel recognizes this because he sees that the judgment God placed on the nation of Israel is about to come to its conclusion (so he thinks).

Daniel is specific in his prayer, admitting that all within Israel (the Jews) have turned aside from God. Because of this guilt, God was right in pouring out His curse. Daniel also recognizes that Israel is without excuse because of what has been written in the Law of Moses.

Israel has nothing to complain about because they got what they were told way ahead of time they *would* get if they ever started doing what they have done. Notice that Daniel is not making one excuse either for himself or the people of Israel. God is just and righteous.

In fact, Daniel points out that though God poured out this curse onto the nation of Israel, this further reveals God's truthfulness because He *said* He would do this if Israel ever broke her covenant with Him.

You see the theme here, don't you? God dealt with Israel exactly as He said He would if they chose to ignore His commands and mandates.

Israel had sunk to the point of worshiping idols and still trying to maintain at least the contrivance of worshiping God. It is impossible to serve God and other gods. We are not made that way and must serve God *or* other gods, but we can never do both.

This reminds me of what we learn in the book of Ezekiel. There God shows Ezekiel how the priests of the Temple had their secret gods which they worshipped, and they did so *right in the Temple area*, in what they thought was the privacy of their own rooms. God saw and He basically explains to Ezekiel rhetorically why He cannot go into His own house of worship (cf. Ezekiel 7:20; all of 8)!

The lunacy seen here is something that we cannot understand, yet if we are honest, we will be forced to admit that we have our own secret vices and gods that we are hard-pressed to give up. We all have our own gods, from money, to work, to church, to family, to comfort, and many other things besides. All of these things in and of themselves are innocuous. It is when we place a high value on them and that value overstates their inherent or real value that we begin to see things as gods.

There is nothing wrong with money, yet it is the *love* of it that is wrong. There is nothing wrong with work, but if we become workaholics, we have fallen into the trap of worshiping our work.

There is nothing wrong with loving family members, but if we place their value above doing God's will, then something is drastically wrong. So it goes with anything we encounter. Most things in and of themselves are not right or wrong. It is when we infuse them with a value they do not have that we tend to begin idolizing them, and that's where the problem lies.

The priests in the Temple thought no one – not even God – could see what they were doing. While pretending to worship the *only* true God, they fell into formal idol worship. This literally pushed God away because they defiled the Temple. Is it any wonder God asks Ezekiel to understand why He (God) could not stay in His own house?

Chapter 5
King Hezekiah

The sad fact is that sometimes, human beings think they know what is best. It is on that basis that we storm the heavens, so to speak, with our requests or even our demands. We think that if we feel so strongly about something, then it must be due to the fact that God wants that something for us.

Because of this, we enter into a time of prayer in which we wind up begging God to do something that He did not intend to do. Such is the case with Hezekiah. This king was near death.

Hezekiah is believed to have been born around 740 BC. He was the son of King Ahaz and Abijah (2 Chronicles 29:1). We learn from 2 Kings 18:1-2 that Abijah was the daughter of the High Priest Zechariah. This should have put Hezekiah in a position of understanding who God is and why God does what He does.

Hezekiah had a fairly long life. As king, he was noted for numerous exploits, not limited to going up against the Assyrian king Sennacherib, the son of Sargon. It was during this time between the death of Sargon and the rule of Sennacherib that Hezekiah attempted to throw off the rule of the Assyrians. While there were wins and losses, Sennacherib ultimately failed to conquer Jerusalem in his attempted retaliation against Hezekiah for no longer wishing to pay tribute.

The Bible tells us that Hezekiah was the first king in the roughly 250 years since Solomon who went into the Temple to pray to God. It was after this that Hezekiah found ways to prepare for the coming onslaught from Sennacherib. He did this by building a wall and a tunnel (cf. Isaiah 33:1; 2 Kings 18:17; 2 Chronicles 32:9; Isaiah 36).

In 2 Kings 20:1-3, we are told, "*In those days was Hezekiah sick unto death. And the prophet Isaiah the son of Amoz came to him, and said unto him, Thus saith the LORD, Set thine house in order; for thou shalt die, and not live.*

"Then he turned his face to the wall, and prayed unto the LORD, saying,

"I beseech thee, O LORD, remember now how I have walked before thee in truth and with a perfect heart, and have done that which is good in thy sight. And Hezekiah wept sore."

Here is a perfect example of a person desiring something that God ultimately saw as not the best route to take. Yet it is clear that God responded to Hezekiah and sent Isaiah back to the king to explain that his prayer had been heard and that he would live another fifteen years.

It always amazes me when people pray to live longer. Obviously, we do this because we have no real grasp of what life is like in the here-*after*. We compare this life to the next and it falls woefully short because we simply cannot adequately picture what the next life is like.

To be sure, those living in the Old Testament times had far less to go on than we do today because we also have the New Testament including the writings of Paul and others who have shed some light on the subject for us. At the same time, we wonder how people could think this life is better than the next.

Such was the case with Hezekiah. He was told he was at the end of his life and didn't want to accept it. He wanted God to fix it, extending his life.

God acquiesced to Hezekiah. He added fifteen years onto the man's life. I'm not sure I would want to know that I had so many years left, would you? Think of it. Every day, you tend to think in terms of how many days, months, or years you have left. We all have death sentences hanging over us and we have no clue when our lives will end. Hezekiah was given that information.

The information about how much longer he would live must have made him a bit giddy. We see this in his actions. He was so overjoyed that he lost his sense of responsibility, paving the way for a neighboring nation to plan when they would come against him to take what was in the king's treasury.

At the word of Isaiah, Hezekiah was healed and granted fifteen more years to live. Unfortunately, this created problems, not only for Hezekiah, but also for his son Manasseh and, ultimately, for Judah.

"At that time Berodachbaladan, the son of Baladan, king of Babylon, sent letters and a present unto Hezekiah: for he had heard that Hezekiah had been sick.

"And Hezekiah hearkened unto them, and shewed them all the house of his precious things, the silver, and the gold, and the spices, and the precious ointment, and all the house of his armour, and all that was found in his treasures: there was nothing in his house, nor in all his dominion, that Hezekiah shewed them not.

"Then came Isaiah the prophet unto king Hezekiah, and said unto him, What said these men? and from whence came they unto thee? And Hezekiah said, They are come from a far country, even from Babylon.

"And he said, What have they seen in thine house? And Hezekiah answered, All the things that are in mine house have they seen: there is nothing among my treasures that I have not shewed them.

"And Isaiah said unto Hezekiah, Hear the word of the LORD.

"Behold, the days come, that all that is in thine house, and that which thy fathers have laid up in store unto this day, shall be carried into Babylon: nothing shall be left, saith the LORD.

"And of thy sons that shall issue from thee, which thou shalt beget, shall they take away; and they shall be eunuchs in the palace of the king of Babylon.

"Then said Hezekiah unto Isaiah, Good is the word of the LORD which thou hast spoken. And he said, Is it not good, if peace and truth be in my days?

"And the rest of the acts of Hezekiah, and all his might, and how he made a pool, and a conduit, and brought water into the city, are they not written in the book of the chronicles of the kings of Judah?

"And Hezekiah slept with his fathers: and Manasseh his son reigned in his stead" 2 Kings 20:12-21.

There are a number of things to note here. First, Hezekiah was indeed healed and was given an additional fifteen years to live. Second, he must have felt so good about it that when the son of the king of Babylon sent his regards, Hezekiah invited the king's messengers to view his treasury. It included silver, gold, spices, precious ointments, armor, and everything else that was valuable to the king.

It seems that Isaiah was a busy prophet with respect to Hezekiah. Note that God sent Isaiah back to Hezekiah to let him know that this thing he had done – showing off the treasury – was going to be his downfall. The Lord was gracious and said through Isaiah that though the king's treasury would be emptied out and carried back to Babylon, it would *not* happen until after the king had died on the fifteenth year.

It was as if Hezekiah had not heard. He was not only careless in showing a neighboring nation what was in the king's treasury, but he seemed to take the same approach with respect to what the Lord had determined would happen. In response to Isaiah Hezekiah says, *"Good is the word of the LORD which thou hast spoken. And he said, Is it not good, if peace and truth be in my days?"*

In essence, the king was saying, "Well, that's great. Nothing bad will happen while I am alive." He did not care what happened after he died. He figured that it would be the problem of the next king, who, as it turned out, was his son Manasseh, who was born during the fifteen years of Hezekiah's extended life!

Manasseh became co-regent with his father Hezekiah when he was but twelve years old and reigned for fifty-five years (cf. 2 Kings 21:1; 2 Chronicles 33:1).

Because his mother was a pagan, Manasseh undid what his father Hezekiah did. While Hezekiah endeavored to rid the southern kingdom of pagan worship, Manasseh brought pagan worship back to the kingdom. He re-initiated pagan worship and undid the religious reforms made by his father Hezekiah.

Hezekiah had destroyed the "brazen serpent" and refused to worship Molech. Through Manasseh, these pagan practices began once again, with Manasseh himself sacrificing his own son to the fires of Molech.

2 Kings 21:16 implies that Manasseh executed those who supported his father's religious reforms. Manasseh was eventually captured by an Assyrian king and imprisoned. *"The severity of Manasseh's imprisonment brought him to repentance. According to one of the two Biblical accounts (2 Kings 21 does not have the account of Manasseh's captivity or repentance), Manasseh was restored to the throne, (2 Chronicles 33:11-13) and abandoned idolatry, removing foreign idols (2 Chronicles 33:15) and enjoining the people to worship in the traditional Israelite manner (2 Chronicles 33:16)."*[2]

Had Hezekiah died when he was originally supposed to have died, a number of things would not have occurred. However, God used the situation to bring Judah captive into their 70 year bondage, spoken of by the prophet Jeremiah. Because of this bondage, we learn of Daniel and the prophecies concerning his people and his holy city, Jerusalem.

Instead of praying to accept God's original decree during his sickness, Hezekiah wept bitterly, begging instead that he be spared. Humanly speaking, no good came from this extension of life. Spiritually, and as far as God was concerned, He brought forth His will in the matter regardless.

---

[2] http://en.wikipedia.org/wiki/Manasseh_of_Judah (January 24, 2012)

What is it about us that makes us think we know better than God does? It is because we see only in part. We cannot see the whole picture from our current human vantage point.

When my sister was literally on her death bed in the hospital, I cried and prayed that God would raise her. I wanted so much for her to get off that bed, go to her home, and continue with life for a while longer.

Instead, God chose to take her to His home, where He had prepared a place for her. The truth is that it took me a good amount of time to accept that decision that God had made.

Once it became clear that God was going to move ahead with His plan to take my sister home, I accepted it. Up to that point, I held out hope that He would raise her from her bed to health.

As I mentioned earlier, I will never forget how the Lord responded to my prayers with respect to my sister's death. It was not His will to give her back to her husband, her son, or me. It was His will to take her home, but within the boundaries of that will, He allowed for one answered prayer that coincided with His perceived will; she opened her eyes.

Once that was done, she closed them, and that evening she slipped away when no one was with her. Yet I have the benefit of knowing that He answered my prayer because it did not go against His revealed will. God is good, and though we do see through an oftentimes very dark glass, God grants us little things that help us grow in our faith toward Him. The purpose of prayer is to give Him thanks, which shows that we trust Him to answer our prayers in a way that is best suited to us. This is the process by which we grow in our faith.

Prayer is designed to let us converse with God. But while we are conversing, the object is to come alongside Him. We are to determine His will through prayer and agree with it.

I'll say it again as I've said it before. God is not our genie. He is not there to grant our physical wishes as they come to us. You want a new car? You want an expensive house? You want, you want, you want? There is a tremendous danger in believing that God is there to do our bidding. We also make a huge mistake in placing emphasis on the things in this life as if they are so extremely important.

We are to yearn for spiritual things. We are to desire those gifts that come from above, not the "gifts" that are here in the physical world.

I have a radio program, and at the end of every show, I sign off with the phrase, "May God open your eyes to see how richly blessed you are in Him." That is my desire not only for myself but for all those who are listening to me. There are certainly physical blessings that God deems wise to provide for us from time to time. However, infinitely more important are those gifts from the spiritual realm. These gifts cannot be measured or valued, for they are limitless in value.

We need to understand that prayer is a two-way street. We give up our will in order that we can readily adopt His will. That is prayer. Anything else is a poor imitation.

Chapter 6

Anguish in Gethsemane

As we look at the unfolding drama of redemption which took place just prior to the arrest, illegal trials, and execution of Jesus, we see the perfect example of what it means to exchange one's will for God's. What we see is a very painful, yet perfect example of how to give up our own desires in order that we might adopt His. Let's take some time to look at the drama itself as it played out.

Luke is the perfect person to record the drama that occurred in the Garden of Gethsemane. Being a doctor, he would understand the medical situation in which blood seeped out of our Lord's forehead.

The scene in Gethsemane on the night Jesus was betrayed proves how excruciating prayer can be at times. What I mean by that is simple. Looking to Jesus as our example, we see just how difficult it can be to give up our will in exchange for God's.

Why was it so difficult? Why so brutal? What was it that caused Him to sweat drops of blood? He was obviously in physical and emotional agony. The situation was made difficult because of the fact that He was literally fighting with Himself to accept only the Father's will and not His own.

In His humanity, Jesus was tempted to want to go the safest, shortest route in following the Father's will. This is how we are all tempted. He'd been tempted on numerous occasions, most notably the time in the wilderness (recorded in Matthew 4) just after He had been baptized.

For forty days He communed with the Father, and at the end of that time, the Tempter came to Him because he knew Jesus would be hungry. Jesus was tempted to turn stones into bread. He refused, responding with Scripture.

The Tempter tried to persuade Jesus to kill Himself. Jesus again refused and again responded with Scripture. On the third try, Satan threw caution to the wind and tried to make a deal with Jesus: worship him (Satan), and in exchange for it, Jesus would gain the world's kingdoms. Once again Jesus refused, responding to the enemy of our souls with Scripture.

These temptations were likely not easy to deal with because of His weakened physical state. Having no food for such a long time, Jesus would have been very hungry and emotionally as well as physically very weak. The Tempter knew that this would be a great time to attack and did so. Let this be a lesson to us. Oftentimes, when we are at our weakest the Tempter comes with suggestions to circumvent

God's Will and/or moral law. It is our choice to either stand with Christ, depending upon His strength to override the Tempter's snares, or to use our free will to give in and follow the dictates of the Tempter.

This is the situation that Jesus faced in the Garden of Gethsemane. He was tempted to circumvent God's established will. We don't know what part of the entire scene was causing such emotional upheaval in Jesus. We simply know that something did cause it, and His reaction to it was to sweat drops of blood.

The turmoil within must have been great for Jesus, yet He persevered in prayer until that moment when He was able to successfully give the entire matter to the Father. This is a lesson we also must learn, and unfortunately, at times we do not learn it well enough.

However, even when we learn it once, another different situation comes along, forcing us to once again trust in God and lay that situation at the feet of our nail-scarred Lord for Him to deal with. By placing our situations at His feet, trusting Him to do what He will do based on the perfection of His will, we grow in Him and we learn what it means to live a faith-rest life.

"And he was withdrawn from them about a stone's cast, and kneeled down, and prayed,

"Saying, Father, if thou be willing, remove this cup from me: nevertheless not my will, but thine, be done.

"And there appeared an angel unto him from heaven, strengthening him.

"And being in an agony he prayed more earnestly: and his sweat was as it were great drops of blood falling down to the ground." (Luke 22:41-44)

Note in the above text that Jesus' turmoil was so great that He wound up sweating ("*His sweat as it were*") blood. This is a true medical condition that can occur with people under tremendous stress. The text does *not* say that it was *like* His sweat was blood. It says, "as it were," meaning it *was blood* with sweat. In either case, He was greatly troubled.

There is tremendous import in this situation. Jesus is facing a *known* and understood future, a future that will cause several things to happen:

1. He will be treated as if He was actually *sin*
2. His Father will turn His back on Jesus, His Son
3. The pain of death will be extreme

So what was it that caused the tremendous stress? Very likely all of it! Jesus was God but also fully human, and He reacted to things as humans do. The only difference (aside from His deity) is the fact that He did not have a sin nature, and because of that, he had never sinned. This fact created within Him the abject horror of having to actually *be* seen as sin, when no sin existed within Him...*ever*.

Yet the writer of Hebews tells us that for the joy set before Him, He endured the cross (Hebrews 12:2). Jesus knew, of course, that because of His actions, multitudes would be blessed and come to be known by Him as His brothers and sisters: the Church.

Once Jesus fully confronted the temptation to go another route, He was at peace because He had fully given up His own desires. This is what He meant when He prayed, "*nevertheless not my will, but thine, be done.*" This is what all Christians must do on a daily basis because that is what Jesus did on a daily basis. He was constantly tempted – as we are – to do His own thing, but it is only through prayer that we are able to give to God our own desires so that in their place He can place His.

I firmly believe that as we grow in our relationship with Christ, we will desire His will more and more and it will become easier to rid ourselves of the things that stand opposed to God. Even with those things that seem to be fine in and of themselves we may find that at a particular time, that is not what God wants for us.

Are you willing to give Him everything? You can only do that through prayer.

Are you dealing with difficult situations in your life? Are you having problems with people? Do you find that it seems as though you are hemmed in on all sides? If so, REJOICE! This is God trying to get your attention. Turn to Him. Spend some time with Him in prayer so that He can rid you of the things which weigh you down.

God knows that the safest place you and I can be is in the center of His will. That only happens when we give up the things that are keeping us from being there.

What is it you need to get rid of? What do you need to give up in order to gain His peace? The thing you are holding onto may be fine in and of itself, but can you give it up to Him?

There is nothing in your life (or mine) that cannot be given to Him. What I mean by that is that we give up *control* of it. We acknowledge that we cannot control circumstances and that He is Lord of all.

Let's say you get fired from a job through no fault of your own. Could you have done anything to prevent it? Probably not, because it likely took you by surprise. If that's the case, then you did not know about it previous to its occurring; however, God did know it and may have personally designed it for you. At the very worst, He allowed it to happen.

I'm sure that when Joseph was sold into slavery by his brothers, he questioned the whole thing. Scripture says that he cried and pleaded

(Genesis 37) with his brothers, but to no avail. They wanted him gone.

Years later – nearly 20 – Joseph faced his brothers once again and essentially told them that what they had meant for evil, God had meant for good. We tend to view things circumstantially. We see what happens and we wonder why. Instead of looking beyond situations (through faith), we tend to focus on the situations themselves, and this keeps us from letting go of them.

By letting go I mean that we should release them *emotionally*. If you get fired and are angry with your employer, you are not trusting God. I'm not saying it's easy. I'm saying that we must pray until we can release the situation. If it returns, we must pray to release it again.

It probably took Joseph some time to do that. Then, after he was purchased as a slave, he wound up in Potiphar's house and was falsely accused of raping Potiphar's wife! He then wound up in prison where he languished for two years. Though Joseph found favor in the jailer's eyes (due to God's blessing with Joseph), he still served a two-year sentence from a crime of which he was innocent!

But after all was said and done, God made Joseph second in command. The only person higher than Joseph in all of Egypt was Pharaoh himself!

Twenty years later, Joseph realized why God had "sent him" (Joseph) ahead of his brothers to Egypt. It was to spare their lives. Now, God certainly could have done things differently, but He chose to do it that way. Why? Probably because there were things in Joseph's life that God needed to help Joseph get rid of, and quite possibly one of those things was arrogance. He likely had a bit of a swollen head from those dreams he kept bragging about to his brothers and father.

There is not one person who ever lives who is free from temptations. Like Jesus, we must pray until we can leave it at the altar and be free from it emotionally. If we don't do that, we are simply carrying it around with us, and because we normally don't have a clue as to why some things happen, we can become embittered. This stems from thinking we know better than God knows.

Jesus worked hard to give up what He knew He had to give up. Even though part of His prayer obviously shows that He wanted something else other than the path before Him, in the end, He gave up His will entirely in favor of the Father's. Jesus overcame the temptation. He never faltered, never sinned. He was tempted but won the victory because He finally got to the point where He said, "*not my will, but thine be done.*" That is the reality of prayer. It is found in giving our will to God in exchange for His will.

Chapter 7
Paul's Prayers

Paul's prayers are often found interwoven throughout his many letters of the New Testament. This gives us some great insight into how the apostle thought and how he prayed, what he viewed as spiritually important and what were the types of things he was willing to let go. In his prayers, we find great insight. Let's take a look.

Paul had a great deal to say about prayer, even highlighting the way in which he prayed for fellow believers. Certainly, it is important for us to know how this man prayed and why he prayed at all.

His letters are filled with bits of prayer scattered here and there. He often began these letters with a brief prayer for the folks he was writing to. For instance, in his letter to the Ephesians, he began with the words:

"Grace be to you, and peace, from God our Father, and from the Lord Jesus Christ.

Blessed be the God and Father of our Lord Jesus Christ, who hath blessed us with all spiritual blessings in heavenly places in Christ." (Ephesians 1:2-3)

Here, Paul is essentially praying out loud for the recipients of his letter. He reminds them as well that we as authentic believers are truly blessed with all spiritual blessings in heavenly places in Christ.

This is a type of prayer: a prayer that we will recognize our blessings in Christ. Paul was a man of prayer and prayed constantly for many things that would benefit the Christian.

He prayed for people to live godly lives. We see this in Scriptures like 2 Corinthians 13:7, which says, *"Now I pray to God that ye do no evil; not that we should appear approved, but that ye should do that which is honest, though we be as reprobates."* Notice how this prayer is also an admonition to do what is right.

Paul echoed this sentiment in other letters he wrote. In his letters like 2 Corinthians 13:9, Philippians 1:9-11, and Colossians 1:9-10, he tells his readers that he is praying for them to walk in a way that pleases the Lord.

How do our prayers measure up? Do we find ourselves praying as Paul prayed, or do we find ourselves praying mainly for our own wants?

In Paul's first letter to the Thessalonian believers, Paul says, *"And the Lord make you to increase and abound in love one toward another, and toward all men, even as we do toward you: To the end he may stablish your hearts unblameable in holiness before God, even our Father, at the coming of our Lord Jesus Christ with all his saints"* (1 Thessalonians 3:12-13). Paul's focus was that each and every Christian should grow in love–love for the Lord and love for His people.

He wanted all Christians to walk in holiness before the Lord because this is our calling. This is who we are as authentic Christians.

Paul also prayed for success in ministry. By that, he did not mean that he was after *worldly* success, as many in ministry today believe they have a right to attain. He was talking about evangelistic areas–that people would respond to the gospel. He also prayed for spiritual success for believers.

In Romans 1:9-11, Paul says, *"For God is my witness, whom I serve with my spirit in the gospel of his Son, that without ceasing I make mention of you always in my prayers; Making request, if by any means now at length I might have a prosperous journey by the will of God to come unto you. For I long to see you, that I may impart unto you some spiritual gift, to the end ye may be established."*

Paul's concern for the believers in Rome was that he would be able to get there and, in the end, be a spiritual blessing for them. Notice how Paul indicates that he prays without ceasing for those believers. Do we? Do we persevere in prayer?

Ephesians 6:19 provides us with knowledge of Paul's desire for his evangelistic efforts: *"And for me, that utterance may be given unto me, that I may open my mouth boldly, to make known the mystery of the gospel."* Do we pray that? Are we more concerned about our own situation than the gospel going out to the lost?

Paul also prayed for strength and a greater knowledge and understanding of God through His Word. Colossians 1:10-11 states, *"That ye might walk worthy of the Lord unto all pleasing, being fruitful in every good work, and increasing in the knowledge of God; Strengthened with all might, according to his glorious power, unto all patience and longsuffering with joyfulness."*

Again, measuring our prayers against Paul's, is this how we pray? Do we want greater strength, greater knowledge, and an increase in patience, even accepting problems with joy? This is how Paul prayed.

"That the God of our Lord Jesus Christ, the Father of glory, may give unto you the spirit of wisdom and revelation in the knowledge of him" (Ephesians 1:17). The more we study Paul's mini-prayers, the more we come to understand just how important prayer truly is, and we cannot live without it.

However, it is important to understand the true nature of prayer, that it is not something for us to simply use to benefit ourselves materially. We need to come to terms with the fact that prayer is our lifeline to the throne for the purpose of separating ourselves from our SELF.

Among the many things for which Paul prayed, love was high on the list. *"And this I pray, that your love may abound yet more and more in knowledge and in all judgment"* (Philippians 1:9). This prayer is from Paul's heart. He desired so much that love would become the norm for Christians and that it would grow and grow.

Paul is not talking about a love that ignores wrongdoing or simply makes someone feel good. He is talking about a love that is from God Himself. The letter to the Philippians is about how Jesus gave up all He had, clothing Himself with humanity in order that He might live among us sinlessly. When it came time to die, He did so humbly, wanting only the Father's will in the matter just as He had successfully sought and fulfilled the Father's will in all other matters.

Paul admonished his readers to live as Jesus lived: a life of love that put God first, others second, and self last. This is why love is so important; it moves us away from SELF. Anyone who can do this easily may need to check their own dedication to the Lord because it is not easy. At every turn, SELF cries out for its own needs to be met.

We are to exemplify Jesus at every turn, who turned aside from His own SELF in order to fulfill the will of His (and our) heavenly Father. This comes through truly loving biblically.

Paul prayed for many things. Chief among them was that Christians should be united in their love for the Lord and for one another. This does not mean that no notice is given to correct theology. It is *because* we love God that we want to know the truth of His Word and are willing to defend that truth. Too many people believe love is simply getting along in spite of major of doctrinal differences. The problem is that if we are not careful, error will work its way into the church we attend. If left unchecked, it will work like leaven, affecting the entire body of believers.

Just as we need to be diligent in love, Paul says that we need to know God better (Ephesians 1:17). The more we get to know the Lord through His Word, the more we will want to protect and defend it lovingly but firmly.

Paul's life as a Christian was filled with knowledge and understanding of God and His Word as well as prayer for other Christians, that they might come along with Him as they sought to know God better. Paul's example is an example we would do well to heed.

Chapter 8
James Weighs In

James is profound, yet poignant, about the way we should pray. I also believe he has been misunderstood. He says, *"Confess your faults one to another, and pray one for another, that ye may be healed. The effectual fervent prayer of a righteous man availeth much,"* (James 5:16).

It is sometimes taught that if we pray in faith, God will always deliver us from calamity or sickness. The problem with that is that we would then have to argue that neither Jesus nor Paul had real faith. God never promises to relieve us of our problems. He only promises to never give us more than we can bare and that He will always provide enough faith through the situation so that we can overcome to the temptation and run away from it.

We could almost say that where Paul is much more spiritually-minded, James deals with where the rubber meets the road.

Where Paul says that we should pray in all things and even pray without ceasing, James tells us to count it all joy when many trials and temptations come our way (cf. James 1:2), because all of these things create a true spiritual attitude in the authentic Christian.

Through these trials and problems we will learn patience if we lean on God. James also realizes that sometimes believers will have a difficult time in certain situations. When that occurs, we should ask God to give us wisdom. *"If any of you lack wisdom, let him ask of God, that giveth to all men liberally, and upbraideth not; and it shall be given him"* (James 1:5).

If you find yourself in a situation where you simply do not know what to do, you should pray to God for wisdom and He will provide it, with the proviso that you ask in faith (v.6). Without faith, it is impossible to please God (Hebrews 11:6). God is there to help us live His will. He doesn't expect us to do it on our own. He is more than willing and able to provide us with insight and wisdom so that we know how to continue in faith through the many trials that this world can and will throw at us.

Again, James emphasizes the fact that we should be doing what the Word teaches. *"Wherefore lay apart all filthiness and superfluity of naughtiness, and receive with meekness the engrafted word, which is able to save your souls. But be ye doers of the word, and not hearers only, deceiving your own selves. For if any be a hearer of the word, and not a doer, he is like unto a man beholding his natural face in a glass: For he beholdeth himself, and goeth his way, and straightway forgetteth what manner of man he was"* (James 1:21-24).

Do you see how Paul and James represent two sides of the same coin? Paul references how we should pray and James deals with what our life looks like (or should) when we pray effectively to live a life that pleases God.

For James, "*Pure religion and undefiled before God and the Father is this, To visit the fatherless and widows in their affliction, and to keep himself unspotted from the world*" (James 1:27). This is religion at work, the result of praying effectively and knowing God through His Word. Paul would agree with this sentiment from James. There is nothing contradictory here at all. Paul is focusing on the prayer life of an authentic believer. James is focusing on the literal walk of the authentic believer – what it looks like to others.

James spends a good amount of time in his letter explaining what the authentic Christian life looks like, and he provides many examples of it along the way so that his readers will understand it. If we only had Paul's letters, we might be tempted to think only in terms of the ethereal, but together with James' letter, we can get a full understanding of what it means to pray as a Christian and what it means to live as one based on the type of praying that the authentic Christian is involved in.

Probably one of the most well known statements from James is this: "*For as the body without the spirit is dead, so faith without works is dead also*" (James 2:26). A person can have all the faith in the world, but if it is not put to good use – the kind of good that brings glory to God – than it really has little value. Faith is the vehicle through which we bring glory to God, whether in our prayers or in our practice.

Chapter 9

Jude Speaks; Jesus Prays

I Jude's short letter is packed with spiritual truths. Among his opening sentences, we find this brief prayer: "*Mercy unto you, and peace, and love, be multiplied*" (Jude 1:2). This echoes Paul's sentiments as well.

Jude wants us to know just how much we are loved and at peace with God because of what Jesus has done for us. Again, though, Jude takes the time to note how apostates have snuck in and begun to create problems for the church.

Much of Jude's letter is a warning to those living during his time and a warning to those who will be the last generation prior to the end of human history. Because of that, there are some very practical applications to the spiritual tone of his letter. Jude's letter represents where the rubber meets the road.

Jesus' prayers often highlight the ethereal bond reflected in His relationship with the Father. This is what Paul often emphasizes.

Often referred to as the great high priestly prayer, the Bible provides us with a tremendous look into the spiritual insight provided by Jesus through one of His prayers. John records the prayer for us in the seventeenth chapter of the gospel bearing his name.

Jesus speaks in the third person here in referring to Himself. As we read it, we are reminded of the passage from Philippians 2, in which Paul describes the emptying that Jesus went through in becoming human. While retaining His deity, Paul tells us that He clothed Himself with humanity. In essence, He became *like* us in order to live *for* us.

While on earth, the only time His attributes of deity were used was when they coincided with the Father's will. The first part of this prayer attests to the fact that Jesus existed prior to becoming human (v.4-5). Here we learn that Jesus existed with the Father before He came to earth in human form, born of young Mary.

"1These words spake Jesus, and lifted up his eyes to heaven, and said, Father, the hour is come; glorify thy Son, that thy Son also may glorify thee:

2As thou hast given him power over all flesh, that he should give eternal life to as many as thou hast given him.

3And this is life eternal, that they might know thee the only true God, and Jesus Christ, whom thou hast sent.

4I have glorified thee on the earth: I have finished the work which thou gavest me to do.

⁵And now, O Father, glorify thou me with thine own self with the glory which I had with thee before the world was."

What is amazing in verse five above is the fact that Jesus attests to the fact that He not only existed with the Father, but it's clear that He and the Father are *one*. Jesus is asking the Father to glorify Him (Jesus). This is clearly a nod to the fact that the Trinity exists.

As followers of Jesus, we do not pray that prayer. The Father *never* glorifies us; however, Jesus asked that He glorify Him (Jesus) which says something tremendously dramatic. Obviously, the two Persons shared a common glory. Jesus set that aside (refusing to use it unless it coincided with the Father's will) when He clothed Himself with humanity. That is absolutely amazing when you stop to consider it. In essence, Jesus was saying that He was *equal* to the Father, though their roles have always been different.

" ⁶I have manifested thy name unto the men which thou gavest me out of the world: thine they were, and thou gavest them me; and they have kept thy word.

⁷Now they have known that all things whatsoever thou hast given me are of thee.

⁸For I have given unto them the words which thou gavest me; and they have received them, and have known surely that I came out from thee, and they have believed that thou didst send me."

Here Jesus states that whatever He was supposed to say and teach the apostles, He did. Note also that they became convinced of Jesus' origin and authority. They knew He came from the Father and was not born into humanity as a human being *only*.

" ⁹I pray for them: I pray not for the world, but for them which thou hast given me; for they are thine.

¹⁰And all mine are thine, and thine are mine; and I am glorified in them.

¹¹And now I am no more in the world, but these are in the world, and I come to thee. Holy Father, keep through thine own name those whom thou hast given me, that they may be one, as we are."

Notice please that Jesus at this point in His prayer is not praying for the entire world, but for these specific men. Note also that Jesus is saying that the Father gave Jesus these men and Jesus has given them back to the Father for His safekeeping.

"¹²While I was with them in the world, I kept them in thy name: those that thou gavest me I have kept, and none of them is lost, but the son of perdition; that the scripture might be fulfilled."

Jesus was able to keep "them in thy name" through prayer and teaching. I imagine that Jesus heavily undergirded these men with prayer – prayer for their growth and prayer for their safety, along with prayer that the world would not overcome them. Do we pray enough? Can we *ever* pray enough?

"¹³And now come I to thee; and these things I speak in the world, that they might have my joy fulfilled in themselves.

¹⁴I have given them thy word; and the world hath hated them, because they are not of the world, even as I am not of the world.

¹⁵I pray not that thou shouldest take them out of the world, but that thou shouldest keep them from the evil."

Here is proof that though we are in the world, we are not of the world. Though Jesus is still talking about the apostles here, the reality is that all authentic Christians are not of this world. All true believers have a citizenship that is far removed from this earth. Notice please that Jesus does not pray that the world would not hate His followers. In fact, He recognizes that the world *will* hate His followers. That's a given, and even with that knowledge Jesus does not ask the Father to remove them from this world but simply to protect them from evil (or from the evil one).

All true Christians will face trials and some will face trials unto death. As I write this, many Christians in various parts of the world are facing persecution and death solely due to the fact that they are believers. This is a fact of our existence here on this planet because this planet is governed to a large extent by the enemy of our souls.

In essence, we are in the enemy camp and he doesn't like it. God protects us, but that is no guarantee that bad things will not happen to us.

"*[16]They are not of the world, even as I am not of the world.*

[17]Sanctify them through thy truth: thy word is truth.

[18]As thou hast sent me into the world, even so have I also sent them into the world.

[19]And for their sakes I sanctify myself, that they also might be sanctified through the truth.

[20]Neither pray I for these alone, but for them also which shall believe on me through their word;

[21]That they all may be one; as thou, Father, art in me, and I in thee, that they also may be one in us: that the world may believe that thou hast sent me."

Here Jesus begins praying for those beyond the original apostles. He prays that we would be one with God in purpose, thought, word, and deed. Jesus is not saying that we will be "one" with the Father even as He is one with the Father. He states instead that just as the Father is "in" Him (Jesus), those who follow Him in truth might also be one with God in mind, spirit, and purpose.

"²²And the glory which thou gavest me I have given them; that they may be one, even as we are one:

²³I in them, and thou in me, that they may be made perfect in one; and that the world may know that thou hast sent me, and hast loved them, as thou hast loved me.

²⁴Father, I will that they also, whom thou hast given me, be with me where I am; that they may behold my glory, which thou hast given me: for thou lovedst me before the foundation of the world."

Another nod to the fact that Jesus existed prior to being born, prior to the Creation of the world and all it contains. Jesus prays that we will be with Him, and we will. As each believer dies, we are present with Jesus. Eventually, all believers will be with Jesus.

"²⁵O righteous Father, the world hath not known thee: but I have known thee, and these have known that thou hast sent me.

²⁶And I have declared unto them thy name, and will declare it: that the love wherewith thou hast loved me may be in them, and I in them" (John 17).

The high priestly prayer of Jesus clues us into Jesus' complete humility. It helps us understand just how Jesus prayed and what was important to Him. The reality is that this is how we should pray, at least in part, because some things we cannot relate to and that is due to His position as Creator and God.

Being one in spirit with other Christians is something we can achieve. Of course, that can only be achieved through the indwelling presence of the Holy Spirit.

Jesus' prayer opens our eyes to the fact that all things are under His immutable control. It shows His deep care, concern, and love for us. Do not miss that He wants us to be with Him. He wants us out of this world, a world controlled by the devil and his angels.

One day, after He opens the seven-sealed scroll of Revelation 5, Jesus will reign over this world. This title deed to earth is what grants Him the ability to rule over the world from His father David's throne.

Don't gloss over this prayer, and note especially the last verse of John 17. Jesus says that He has declared the Father's Name unto His followers and He will continue to declare it through followers who came after those first century followers. He so wants us to know His love, that this love may be the hallmark of Christians everywhere.

Chapter 10
Why and When Should We Pray?

There are any number of reasons we should pray, but the one that is likely most important in my estimation is that prayer is literally *communing with God*. There is something to be said about that; the created speaking with the Creator.

Because of this fact, is it any wonder that Paul speaks about praying without ceasing (Ephesians 6:18)? I've been married for just over twenty-five years and I cannot imagine ignoring my wife. The idea of not talking to her about this or that doesn't enter into the picture.

Most of us have a good friend (and if you're married, I hope it's your spouse). Because we enjoy their company, we like to be around them. We enjoy discussing things, things that they will find important simply because we are saying them.

Being in a quality relationship takes work, and it takes time to develop. Those who stop talking to one another usually find a way to the door. They leave and don't come back. Normally, two people who have stopped speaking no longer have a relationship.

Can you imagine if you only spoke to a good friend when you needed something? You're worried about a situation at work, so you need to run things past them to get their input. Maybe you're bothered by something, so you need their support. Maybe you wind up using your friend as a sounding board. If that is the extent of the relationship you have with another person, then that, my friend, is no relationship at all. It's one-sided and destructive. Soon the other person will grow tired of literally being used and will look for the nearest door.

All people want to be loved. It's the way we are made. God wants us to love Him as well. We are not showing our love for Him if all we do is present our requests to Him. We need to do that because He *is* our Father, but we also need to spend time simply praising Him for all that He has done for us.

We should pray whenever we think of it. Do you need to be reminded to talk to your spouse or good friend? Hopefully it comes naturally. If it doesn't, there truly is a problem. Our conversation with God (and that's exactly what it is) should be as natural as discussing anything with a loved one.

When should we pray? Often, but we need to get past the idea of thinking that prayer is merely me talking *to* God. I've already mentioned what it would be like if we only talked with a friend when we had something to say and did not really care whether or not they had anything to say back to us. We want their ear so we talk. We have something on our heart, so we vent. This is part of a working relationship, but it is not the only part.

If prayer for you is relegated to simply *unloading*, then you have not gotten to the real depth in prayer. Prayer must be a two-way street. God needs to speak to us, but I'm not talking about some ethereal, esoteric *feeling* or *experience* where we think we actually hear the voice of God. I'm talking about God speaking to us through His Word. The more familiar you become with God's Word, the more things you will have to pray about.

Have you ever been reading His Word and stopped to ask God why something was there? The other day, I was reading Exodus 29-30 as part of my daily devotion. I came to this phrase: *"And this is the thing that thou shalt do unto them to hallow them,* **to minister unto me** *in the priest's office"* (Exodus 29:1; emphasis added). I find that phrase, "to minister unto me," fascinating, don't you?

God *wants* us to minister to *Him*! Now, in Exodus 29, God describes what the priests should wear and how they should do their duties in the Tabernacle. So the phrase specifically refers to the priests: Aaron and his sons. In the act of fulfilling their priestly obligations, they were actually ministering to God! Consider that and what it means.

When we pray, we can be praying selfishly or we can simply commune (talk) with God. One of things that bugs me is when I hear people leading prayer and their prayer goes something like this: *"Dear Father, please help us to worship you in truth, Father. And Father, may our eyes be open, Father, to that truth, Father, which is found only in your Word, Father. Help us to live lives, Father, that bring glory to you, Father..."*

Do you see what's happening here? Who *talks* like that in normal conversation?! My wife's name is Silvia. I can only imagine how ridiculous it would sound if in the course of conversing with her, I said something like this:

"Silvia, would you mind if we ran some errands now, Silvia? I'd like to go to that store Silvia, then to the other store on the list, Silvia. Silvia, I would also like to hit the grocery store, Silvia, last, because we'll have cold cuts, Silvia, and whatnot that will require refrigeration, Silvia."

Go back and read that aloud to hear how asinine it sounds. This is what we do with God! Why do we do this? It is because we do not understand that He simply wants us to *converse with Him*, as opposed to talking *to* or *at* Him!

Imagine how annoyed your boss would get if you repeated his/her name as many times as I have said the word "Silvia" in the above example. They would wonder why on earth you were doing that, and rightly so.

I used to do this all the time until I realized what I'm sharing with you. People who repeat God's name a lot aren't really talking with God. They are essentially more concerned about how they are coming across to those who are listening. That's the sad fact. To top it off, they may ask someone close to them how their prayer was, as if it's graded.

We need to set pretense aside and simply talk *with* God. We need to do it often, and we shouldn't have to be reminded to do it. This is exactly why we are told to pray without ceasing. Do you have to be reminded to talk to your spouse or good friend? It comes naturally, doesn't it? It should be the exact same way with God. We should want to talk with Him. We should want to dwell on His Word.

If we do not want to do this, then something is wrong and we need to figure out what the problem is before we move on. Don't worry, just ask God to help you figure it out and He will!

How often should we pray?

1 Corinthians 1:4 - *I give thanks to my God always for you because of the grace of God that was given you in Christ Jesus…*

Ephesians 6:18 - *…praying at all times in the Spirit, with all prayer and supplication. To that end keep alert with all perseverance, making supplication for all the saints…*

Philippians 1:3-4 - *I thank my God in all my remembrance of you, always in every prayer of mine for you all making my prayer with joy…*

Colossians 1:3 - *We give thanks to God and the Father of our Lord Jesus Christ, praying always for you…*

1 Thessalonians 5:17 - *…pray without ceasing…*

Chapter 11
How Should We Pray?

Knowing how to pray is important for knowing how to live the Christian life on a daily basis. There are many sections of Scripture that teach us how to pray, and we would do well to learn from them.

Psalm 66:17 - *I cried to him with my mouth, and high praise was on my tongue.*

Notice that David is saying that he cried out to God with praise. That's important to understand. Paul talks about the same thing. We should enter His courts with praise.

Psalm 95:2 - *Let us come into his presence with thanksgiving; let us make a joyful noise to him with songs of praise!*

Again, note the emphasis on praise. There were many times in the life of David before and during his reign as monarch that he was troubled. It caused him to cry out for help, but almost invariably, he would end his Psalm with praise to God for who He is and what He does for those who love Him.

Matthew 6:9-13 - *After this manner therefore pray ye: Our Father which art in heaven, Hallowed be thy name. Thy kingdom come, Thy will be done in earth, as it is in heaven. Give us this day our daily bread. And forgive us our debts, as we forgive our debtors. And lead us not into temptation, but deliver us from evil: For thine is the kingdom, and the power, and the glory, for ever. Amen.*

This prayer is beautiful for its simplicity. The overall focus is on God, and the very first thing the prayer says is that God's Name should be hallowed, or praised. It should be lifted up. God is above all things and is completely separate from His Creation. He should be treated like that as well. Too often, people think they know best.

People want to take God on, to call Him out. The reality is that God laughs at the professed profundity of humanity. *"He that sitteth in the heavens shall laugh: the LORD shall have them in derision. Then shall he speak unto them in his wrath, and vex them in his sore displeasure"* (Psalm 2:4-5).

We should take the time to recognize who God is, and if we do that we will be more willing to humble ourselves before Him. When we begin to come to this point of knowledge, we have begun to arrive indeed.

Note also that we should only be concerned about today – "give us this day our daily bread." We are not to be concerned about tomorrow. This does not mean we cannot make plans. It means we should not inordinately be concerned about what will happen tomorrow, how we will react to things, and how all of it will affect us. We should deal with it when it arrives by giving things to Him. To busy ourselves with concerns for a day that has not even arrived yet means we are wasting the day we are living in. We should live in the here and now, not the then and tomorrow.

We should pray with the belief that God is guiding our lives. He wants to guide us into areas that will bring us growth and Him glory. This is the essence of being a Christian, and the sooner we come to realize it, the sooner we will get to live it.

Our prayers should mirror the way we feel about God. Too often we doubt or grow concerned or angry about a situation, when in reality we should be fully focused on Him and what we can do to reflect His light to a dying world.

Satan wants to enslave us. If he cannot successfully keep us from becoming a Christian, he will do what he can to keep us from walking successfully as an authentic Christian. One of the ways we learn he does this is through temptation. God does not lead us into temptation, but Satan does. We should pray that we are not led into temptation and for God to deliver us from all evil. Again, this does not mean that evil will never touch our lives. Ultimately, God will deliver us from all of it, even if that means that He uses death to accomplish it, as in the case of martyrdom.

Chapter 12
For What Should We Pray?

It is easy to see and use prayer merely as a direct request line to the throne in which we seek to have all of our wants fulfilled by the Living God. There are too many people teaching this type of "theology" today, and unfortunately, because of it, too many believe it. God is not our genie. He does not sit on His glorious throne in heaven desperately waiting for His children to make their requests known to Him so that He will provide them with every whim, every wish. Yes, we are to make our requests known to God, but those requests need to fall in line with His will, not ours.

If you are the type of person who simply comes to God when there is a problem in your life or when you want something new that you do not have, I would implore you to rethink your understanding of prayer.

The difficult part of prayer is in the not knowing. Anyone will tell you that. We know that we need to have faith. We know that we need to see through the darkness of not knowing to faith, believing that God will answer according to His will. We also know there is so much that we are unable to discern about prayer.

The Bible tells us much, and if not studied thoroughly, we could end up with the wrong impression about prayer. By taking verses out of context, it is easy to arrive at a conclusion that says God will heal sickness every time. We can erroneously believe that God wants to bless me *materially* in this life. There are many conclusions we can draw about prayer that are far from its reality.

Questions concerning prayer arise that are difficult to answer. We look at the book of Job, for instance, and we see a man – Job – who was righteous. Yet in spite of that, God allowed Job to be tested and tested *severely* by the enemy of our souls.

We learn from Job's experience that Satan has tremendous power, and that power is kept in check by God alone. In essence, then, Satan can use whatever means is necessary to overcome a believer, even temporarily, if allowed to do so by God.

We learn from Daniel that persistence in prayer pays off. We know that he prayed for 21 days for an answer to prayer (cf. Daniel 9), yet on the first day he prayed, the angel Gabriel was sent to provide an answer to Daniel. Unfortunately, Gabriel was delayed in coming. Why the delay? We learn that a prince of Persia – likely a powerful demonic entity – kept this godly messenger at bay for three weeks. There are spiritual beings more powerful than some of God's own angels.

All the while Daniel knew nothing of this supernatural battle that was taking place in the heavenly realms. He was unaware of how real it was and of the need for Michael the Archangel to come and help the messenger so that he could carry the answer to Daniel. Had Gabriel not explained the reason for the delay, not only Daniel, but we too would still be in the dark.

So why did God allow Gabriel to be so accosted and kept at bay for three weeks, only finding his freedom to continue on to Daniel after Michael fought for his release? If we look at the truth of Daniel 9, we see the importance of that particular passage. In fact, it is the only passage in all of Scripture that deals with the 70 weeks and the details noted therein by Gabriel.

The 70 weeks are directly connected to the nation of Israel and are extremely important. They tell of the times of the Gentiles and how Jerusalem and the Holy Mount (Temple Mount) will be trodden under the feet of Gentile nations until the end of human-led history.

Moreover, this period of time details the rise of the Antichrist and the final seven years of human history known as the Tribulation. It was because of Daniel's righteous prayers that he was heard and an answer to his questions given.

With this knowledge, is it any wonder that the prince of Persia did not want Gabriel to arrive to Daniel with the answer to his prayers? Of *course* he would do his best to keep that answer from arriving, even if it meant keeping Gabriel at bay for as long as possible. Once Michael arrived, the prince of Persia was overcome, which allowed Gabriel to go on his way.

I also think it is telling that Gabriel knew that upon his return to the throne he would again be hammered by another prince (demonic entity) who would attempt to keep him from getting back to the throne.

What this tells me is that not all angels are alike. Some are certainly far more powerful than others. Is this why Jesus tells us to be persistent in prayer (cf. Luke 18:1-8)? This seems to be the case. There is something about persistent, consistent prayer that rises to the throne. Maybe it has to do with the fact that the angels who carry our prayers to God's throne are often accosted along the way.

But this brings us to another question. Can God not hear our prayers until the angel relays the message? Of course He can, without doubt. However, there is a procedure that God has obviously put into place that captures our prayers and guides them to the throne of grace.

So if it takes time for our prayers to get there "physically," what is the purpose of that? There can only be one answer. Faith. It is to build up our faith in God and His ability to hear and respond to our prayers.

It is tempting to think that Satan has more power than He does. It is tempting to think that our prayers are answered based on our ability to pray persistently. I don't believe this to be the case at all. God uses time to build up our faith just as He did with Daniel. There was no chance that Daniel's prayer had not been answered. It was merely a matter of time until the answer reached Daniel.

In today's day and age, we do not have angels appearing to us with an answer from God's throne. We have the indwelling Holy Spirit who is always before God's throne since He is God as the Father is God and as the Son is God. If the Holy Spirit dwells within us, He not only knows the prayers of our heart but helps us when we don't even *know* how to pray (cf. Romans 8:26; John 14:26; see also Galatians 4:6).

There are situations in our lives that require concerted prayer if for no other reason than to continue to remind us of areas in our life that God needs to have control of and of which we need to let go. There are times when we need to spend time in prayer simply praising Him for His answer to prayer, whether we know what that answer is or not.

Praising God in all things (cf. 1 Thessalonians 5:18) is probably the very best way that I know of to let God have control of circumstances. I've given a few examples of this throughout this book, but there are others.

Recently, I've been praying that God would open doors that seem closed but that it also seems He wants open. I'm not sure what those doors are, but I feel certain that He wants them open. Is it a case of me simply being involved in wishful thinking that God wants something that He does not? Is it a case of spiritual entities fighting against God's will to keep His will from happening?

I believe it is the latter rather than the former. So if that is the case, then what can be better than praising Him for His will, even though it appears to be yet unfulfilled?

When Jesus was in the Garden of Gethsemane on the night He was betrayed, He prayed for options. He presented His request to the Father with the proviso that His and only His will would be done. Jesus had wants, but He *never* allowed those wants to supersede the Father's will in the matter. The fact that Jesus said, "Not mine, but thy will be done," proves this beyond doubt.

In essence, Jesus was able to let go of his wants for the exclusivity of the Father's will. How can human beings do this? Through *praise*. When we give thanks for something we are not particularly happy about, we are in the process of letting the situation go. If we continue to hang onto our wants, either it will appear as though God will not move or He will move to perform His will and we will be unable to accept and receive it.

In the situation that I noted regarding God wanting to open doors for me to walk through, it is my responsibility to praise Him for His will. It is in praising Him that I am able to let go and let God complete His will.

If God wants me to be in a holding pattern, per se, then what is that to me? If God is going to wait months or years before the things He has me praying about come to pass, what is that to me? It is clear then that the length of time before He moves is completely His to ordain. If I get frustrated in the meantime, continuing to think that because God has placed something on my heart, He must mean for it to happen very soon, then I am setting myself up for failure. God does not often tell us ahead of time of His timing. We may get a sense of His timing in general terms, but that may be all. As the time approaches, we may get a sense of things being narrowed down.

Suppose God has me waiting for three years before He opens doors? In the meantime, I'm doing other things that He has prepared for me, so I believe I am still performing His will. If He is preparing me to move in another direction, I must remember that rarely, if ever, does God give us only a one-day notice. More often than not, He gives us plenty of time to become acclimated to the perfection of His will. He knows our frame and that we came from dust. He knows our weaknesses and deficiencies. He brings us along gently, slowly, and consistently. Our job is to trust Him, and once again, the best way to trust Him is through a continual attitude of praise and thanksgiving.

If instead of praying that He will open the doors He plans to open I spend time praising Him for the perfection of His will and the timing of that will, then I am in His will because I am proving to Him that I am trusting Him.

I learned years ago that the best way to prove to God that we are trusting Him is through praise. We may not feel it when we start to praise Him, but this sacrifice of praise will soon turn into a reality that we did not know could exist (cf. Psalm 50:14). It is a sacrifice of praise and thanksgiving when we do not understand and even find it difficult to agree but we praise Him anyway because we believe He knows best.

This is exactly what Jesus did in the Garden of Gethsemane. He essentially thanked God the Father for the perfection of His will and accepted it. It was in the act of saying "Father, not my will but thine be done" that Jesus praised the Father for that will. Jesus knew that the Father's will was best, beyond reason. Though He shrank from the coming trials, pain, and separation from the Father that would befall Him, Jesus ultimately fully submitted Himself to the Father. There is no greater sacrifice. A sacrifice of praise and thanksgiving is something the Lord wants to see in all of His children.

We do not know the path intimately until we get there. The problem, though, is that we often *think* we know better than God about the many situations in our lives. He wants us to forget about our lives, take up our cross, and follow Him on a daily basis. This tells me that He does not want me to be preoccupied with the things that concern my life but to be occupied within the confines of His will.

Satan loves to get our minds on ourselves. He wants us to spend time agonizing over this thing or that with respect to our lives. The problem is that doing this keeps us from spending our lives fully involved in God's will.

So I believe that God wants to open doors. I can spend a good amount of time praying that He would open those doors, or I can spend a good amount of time *praising* Him for the fact that He is going to open doors when He sees fit. So every time I am tempted to think about, dwell on, and even become frustrated about those doors that appear to be closed, I have two choices: I can pray hard that He will open them, or I can offer praise to Him for His will and His timing. By doing the former, I tend to hang onto it. With the latter, I tend to let it go for His safe keeping.

I think what I am describing is what someone has called the "faith-rest" life of a Christian. By offering praise in all things, I am letting go of my wants. I am exercising faith in His ability to get His will accomplished. I am also resting in the fact that doors will open when they are supposed to open. Do you see that? This is the mark of a mature Christian, and I'm certainly not saying I'm there yet or there consistently. I'm saying that is the mark which we strive to reach.

I believe this is the mark that Jesus aimed for and reached in the Garden of Gethsemane. Had he continued to ask God to remove the "cup" from Him without adding the proviso about the Father's will being done, it would have amounted to *sin*. Jesus would have been guilty of putting His will ahead of the Father's will. This is sinful. It stems from our own ego, thinking that we know better than God does.

Of course, Jesus passed the test with flying colors. Though He wanted to shrink from what was to come His way, He submitted Himself perfectly to the Father's will and He knew exactly what that meant in His case.

As Christians, the best of our prayers can be found in praising Him for His will even when our wants to not coincide with that will. I believe there will always be an element of the unknown when it comes to prayer in this life. Paul said we see through a glass darkly (cf. 1 Corinthians 13:12). This is how it is, which is why faith is so important. The best evidence of our faith is in praising Him for those things that we cannot see.

As I said at the beginning of this book, it was not written to be the final word on the subject; however, I hope and pray that you have gained something more about prayer that you did not know prior to reading it. Prayer is infinitely more than simply asking God to do things.

We need to keep in mind that prayer should – at its most primary and basic level – bring us into closer relationship with the God of the universe. The overriding goal with prayer is not to have your will accomplished but to have God's will brought to fruition.

The byline of this book is "exchanging your will for God's," and that is how prayer should be viewed. This by no means intends to say that God will not give us good things, but it goes well beyond this because God has a plan for each person. That plan may or may not coincide with how we normally think in terms of what our life should look like.

If we stop to consider the fact that around the globe there are Christians who are being persecuted for the faith – sometimes to the death – it makes it that much more startling when we come to God and only ask him about things that will make us happy.

Did Jesus do that? Did Paul do that? How about James or Jude? What about Moses? Did Moses ask God for things that made his life easier?

In Exodus 32, we read of a situation that captured the hearts of the Israelites. Moses had been up on the Mount of God for quite some time, and the people became restless. Soon, they went to Aaron and demanded that he make them a god that they could see and worship.

Aaron complied and told the people to give up their gold, thenhe took their gold, melted it, and formed a golden calf. Once that was done, which likely took any number of days, the people burnt sacrifices to the calf, worshiped it and then got up to "play." The word "play" here has sexual overtones to it. They danced and got themselves all riled up.

While still on the Mount of God, and having just received the two tablets written by God Himself (Exodus 31:18), Moses is told by God to go down because the people had corrupted themselves by worshiping other gods. God then tells Moses, "*Now therefore let me alone, that my wrath may wax hot against them, and that I may consume them: and I will make of thee a great nation*" (Exodus 32:10).

Here the LORD tells Moses what He is planning to do to the people because of their sin. Moses wastes no time and jumps right on that by responding with, "*LORD, why doth thy wrath wax hot against thy people, which thou hast brought forth out of the land of Egypt with great power, and with a mighty hand?*

"*Wherefore should the Egyptians speak, and say, For mischief did he bring them out, to slay them in the mountains, and to consume them from the face of the earth? Turn from thy fierce wrath, and repent of this evil against thy people.*

"*Remember Abraham, Isaac, and Israel, thy servants, to whom thou swarest by thine own self, and saidst unto them, I will multiply your seed as the stars of heaven, and all this land that I have spoken of will I give unto your seed, and they shall inherit it for ever*" (Exodus 32:11-14).

The above text is Moses' prayer to God on behalf of the people of Israel. Moses didn't have to intervene at all. He could have sat back and watched the LORD destroy all of Israel in order to start over with Moses. Instead, Moses acted as high priest for the Israelites. He implored the LORD not to do this but instead to blot out his (Moses') name from the book of Life. Note also that Moses pointed out to God how it would look to the Egyptians and other nations. Did God want His own Name to be one of derision?

God did not need to hear any of this. He was testing Moses to see what his response would be. It's not as if Moses told God anything He did not already know. God wanted Moses to experience being in the position of interceding for the people of Israel.

God relented and allowed the people to live. However, 3,000 of them died by the sword that day and God visited a plague upon them as well. Sin has consequences.

The main point of this interaction is *how* Moses prayed to the LORD. Yes, he spoke to God directly on that mount, but that is what prayer is all about. Moses took the time to beseech the LORD so that He would not follow through on His threat to destroy everyone. Moses was concerned about the people of Israel, not himself.

God had already said that He would make a nation out of Moses, so Moses was in the clear. He could have just sat back and waited for the LORD to do what He said He would do. Instead, Moses stood in the gap, interceding for the people of Israel so that God would choose a different path.

Again, all of this was for Moses' growth. In essence, Moses was a prayer warrior for the undeserving people of Israel. This is what we are with respect to prayer when we pray for the lost of this world. We bring them up before God so that He will somehow, some way, open their closed eyes to the truth of the gospel of Jesus Christ.

The people who are lost do not deserve God's salvation. We were *all* in that position at one time, but thanks be to God, someone was probably praying for us, and God chose to respond by opening our blind eyes to the truth. He was under no obligation to do that, but He did, in response to prayer.

My wife and I did the best we knew how with respect to our children. We raised them to be church-goers. We had them in Sunday school.

We bought them Bibles and reminded them to read them. We talked to them about salvation.

In all of this, there was one thing that we could not do and that only God could: open their eyes. We could talk to them until we were blue in the face. Only God could make sense of His gospel to them. We spent time praying for them.

Fortunately, as far as we know, both of our children are saved; our daughter has married a believer and we pray the same for our son. There are certain things that only God can do and He does those things because of His great love for us.

Moses interceded for the people of Israel on numerous occasions. He did so because of his great compassion for them even when he got angry with them.

With respect to the Golden Calf event, neither God nor Moses was happy. After asking who was with the Lord and seeing the Levites respond, Moses commanded that they should go through the camp and kill people. That day 3,000 people died because of their sin.

This was another case of God purging the camp of rebels. People tend to think that those who came out of Egypt with Moses in the lead were all "saved" in that they were all desirous of following the LORD. This is absolutely not the case. There were many among the ranks of the Israelites who were along for the ride because they didn't want to be in Egypt any longer. The work was too difficult and they had to make bricks with virtually no straw. It was backbreaking work that often came up short. They were whipped for their failures, and in a case like that, who would *not* want to be freed from that tyranny?

People like that joined the crowd of other Israelites and headed out of Egypt to the Promised Land. Along the way, those who were only there for the ride were the ones who were constantly complaining and rebelling. Every so often, God had to purge these rebels from the camp.

This is also exactly why some of the laws of the Israelites were so stringent, seemingly without mercy.

In Exodus 31, we learn about the restrictions surrounding the Sabbath Day rest. Here is what God says about the Sabbath:

"Verily my sabbaths ye shall keep: for it is a sign between me and you throughout your generations; that ye may know that I am the LORD that doth sanctify you.

*"Ye shall keep the sabbath therefore; for it is holy unto you: every one that defileth it shall surely **be put to death**: for whosoever doeth any work therein, that soul **shall be cut off** from among his people.*

*"Six days may work be done; but in the seventh is the sabbath of rest, holy to the LORD: whosoever doeth any work in the sabbath day, he **shall surely be put to death**.*

"Wherefore the children of Israel shall keep the sabbath, to observe the sabbath throughout their generations, for a perpetual covenant.

"It is a sign between me and the children of Israel for ever: for in six days the LORD made heaven and earth, and on the seventh day he rested, and was refreshed." (Exodus 31:13b-17; emphasis added)

Note how many times God says that those who do not recognize the Sabbath will be killed or "cut off" (same thing). He isn't kidding. That was the penalty for profaning the Sabbath by doing any work on it.

Generations later, this became surrounded with tradition created by the Pharisees so that people couldn't even pluck the kernels of wheat from the fields without breaking the Sabbath. There was no law that said a person could not pluck the heads of wheat from the field so that they could eat. Eating was allowed on the Sabbath and to pluck a few heads of wheat did not constitute work. That's not the way the Pharisees saw it, though.

God put all the laws into effect so that people would be without excuse. The Sabbath was particularly given to the Jewish people as a covenant sign between them and the LORD. This covenant sign was to be for all generations.

Today, there are Christians who believe the Sabbath must be obeyed. This is not the case, simply because it was clearly given to the Jews. As Christians, we *should* take at least one day out of every week and dedicate it to the LORD, but in essence, *every* day for the Christian is to be sanctified and holy, even those days when we go to work or work in the garden.

In the end, every Christian should pray for God's will to be done in his/her life. It is perfectly summed up in what has become known as the Lord's prayer from Matthew 6:9b-13:

> *Our Father which art in heaven, Hallowed be thy name.*
>
> *Thy kingdom come. Thy will be done in earth, as it is in heaven.*
>
> *Give us this day our daily bread.*
>
> *And forgive us our debts, as we forgive our debtors.*
>
> *And lead us not into temptation, but deliver us from evil: For thine is the kingdom, and the power, and the glory, for ever. Amen.*

Notice that Jesus teaches people a number of things about prayer. First, He notes that we should come into God's presence with *praise*. There are many things for which we can and should praise the Lord, but these are often lost to us because all we are thinking about are the things we think we *need*.

Our prayers should begin with praise to our heavenly Father. Next, we would pray that His Kingdom will come and that His will, which is done perfectly in heaven, should be done that way on earth. One day, it will be so.

Note also that when it comes to our needs, we should take one day at a time: "give us this day our daily bread." This does not mean that we can't pray about things that are coming down the pike (college, marriage partners for our children, etc.), but it does mean that we should not be preoccupied with those things to the exclusion of our basic needs for this particular day.

Notice also that forgiveness – the next subject – is a two-way street. God forgives us and we forgive others. We cannot forgive judicially. We can only arrive at a point where we no longer hold a grudge. Only God forgives us judicially, completely blotting out our sin(s) as if they never occurred. In effect, if we are no longer holding a grudge against someone, then we are treating them the same way God treats us.

The last few lines deal with the fact that God will not lead us into temptation. We do that. The prayer is really asking that we will not allow ourselves to be led into temptation. We need God's help in delivering us from evil, and it's a lot easier to pray about that *before* you find yourself having to deal with a tempting situation.

All power and all glory belong to the Lord. Isaiah tells us that He will share His glory with no one, and who can blame Him? He alone is God. Our lives should be lived so that at every turn, every moment, He receives the glory for the actions, the words, and even the thoughts in our life.

The Lord's Prayer is a beautiful lesson in how to pray. It helps us come to terms with the fact that we are not (or at least *should* not) be the center of our universe.

We are here for a far higher purpose, and that purpose is to bring glory to God.

For what should we pray?

Romans 15:30 - *I appeal to you, brothers, by our Lord Jesus Christ and by the love of the Spirit, to strive together with me in your prayers to God on my behalf...*

2 Corinthians 1:11 - *You also must help us by prayer, so that many will give thanks on our behalf for the blessing granted us through the prayers of many.*

1 Timothy 2:1-2 - *First of all, then, I urge that supplications, prayers, intercessions, and thanksgivings be made for all people, for kings and all who are in high positions, that we may lead a peaceful and quiet life, godly and dignified in every way.*

James 5:13-14 - *Is anyone among you suffering? Let him pray. Is anyone cheerful? Let him sing praise. Is anyone among you sick? Let him call for the elders of the church, and let them pray over him, anointing him with oil in the name of the Lord.*

James 5:16 - *Therefore, confess your sins to one another and pray for one another, that you may be healed. The prayer of a righteous person has great power as it is working.*

For what should we pray? In a nutshell, we should pray for His will in all things. Sometimes I will go for a walk in the morning and use the time to pray. As I was walking not long ago, I realized once again that I was alive for another day – another day that God had planned for me. It was my obligation to pray for wisdom in knowing what His will was for me for that particular day, as in every day.

I could have used the time to pray selfishly for the things I wanted, but I know that as His children who have been bought with a price, we need to understand that His will should be foremost in our lives.

Once we begin to understand that prayer should be used to determine His will, our prayer life will increase. We will no longer be hampered with the things that we think affect only ourselves. We will begin to understand that God's will covers what He wants to do in and through us.

We need to spend time in prayer discovering His will for us for each day we are alive. That's it: learning what He would have us do for that day. This is not to say that He will not also begin to give us a bigger picture of what He's doing in and through us. He will do that, but He starts with helping us understand what He wants to accomplish for that particular day.

This is how Jesus lived. This is how we need to live as well.

Chapter 13

For Whom Should We Pray?

Everyone. That's the short answer. We should pray for everyone and we should pray often.

Romans 15:30 - *I appeal to you, brothers, by our Lord Jesus Christ and by the love of the Spirit, to strive together with me in your prayers to God on my behalf...*

2 Corinthians 1:11 - *You also must help us by prayer, so that many will give thanks on our behalf for the blessing granted us through the prayers of many.*

1 Timothy 2:1-2 - *First of all, then, I urge that supplications, prayers, intercessions, and thanksgivings be made for all people, for kings and all who are in high positions, that we may lead a peaceful and quiet life, godly and dignified in every way.*

James 5:13-14 - *Is anyone among you suffering? Let him pray. Is anyone cheerful? Let him sing praise. Is anyone among you sick? Let him call for the elders of the church, and let them pray over him, anointing him with oil in the name of the Lord.*

James 5:16 - *Therefore, confess your sins to one another and pray for one another, that you may be healed. The prayer of a righteous person has great power as it is working.*

Sometimes God uses our emotions to let us know something is up. I want to be careful here because I do *not* believe we should live our Christian life by our emotions. I'm simply saying that sometimes, our emotions can clue us into something – reacting to a stimulus. For instance, if you sense a sort of restlessness in your soul, the Lord may be using that to grab your attention so that you can pray about it.

I recall Reverend David Wilkerson being used of God to minister to the needs of gang members in New York City years ago. Out of that came the book *The Cross and the Switchblade* and the conversion of Nicky Cruz, gang leader to the notorious MauMau gang.

Prior to going to New York City, Rev. Wilkerson sensed a certain restlessness in his soul. There was no earthly reason for it, but it appeared that God wanted to get his attention. Because of that, he was led to head to New York City where he began preaching on the street corners.

This was a case of God creating a sense of restlessness in order to get Wilkerson's attention. It worked. Wilkerson devoted himself to prayer and the resultant sense he got was that he was to go from rural Pennsylvania to urban New York City to preach the gospel.

God will use whatever is at His disposal to get our attention. Unusual or unexplainable restlessness can be the trigger that God will use to cause us to turn to Him in exerted prayer. As I write this, I myself am experiencing a sense of restlessness that is causing me to pray to Him, but I really have no clue as to why I am experiencing it. It could be as simple as the enemy doing his best to thwart God's plan in and through me, and God wants me to pray for peace, safety, and the ability to overcome.

Recall the time that Jesus said to Peter that Satan wanted to sift him (Peter) as wheat. *"And the Lord said, "Simon, Simon! Indeed, Satan has asked for you, that he may sift you as wheat. But I have prayed for you, that your faith should not fail; and when you have returned to Me, strengthen your brethren"* (Luke 22:31-32)

Our Lord knew that Satan was going to attack Peter. He also knew that Peter would succumb. Jesus had prayed for Peter and knew he would return. The next few verses tell us *how* Satan was attempting to sift Peter. Peter was going to deny the Lord three times before the cock crowed, and that is exactly what happened. Yet even after such a great fall, Peter returned.

There is much that goes on in the spiritual realm, and we're not aware of most of it. Both demons and angels flit to and fro accomplishing the will of their respective masters. We really have no clue as to how often they come near us, either tempting us to ignore God's will, in the case of demons, or helping us to accomplish it, in the case of angels.

We cannot actually see how Satan works or what his minions do to cause us to fall away in sinful activity. We do not know how the angels work to help us and keep us from stumbling. We've only seen glimpses into that realm in God's Word, and that's all we have.

We know how Satan attacked Jesus in Matthew 4, just after His public water baptism. We know that He used and distorted God's Word as he always does to try to get Jesus to falter. It didn't work. Unfortunately, his tactics too often work with us because we are not as zealous as Jesus was when He lived on this planet. We do not know the Word as well as He did because He was and remains the Word of God.

We know that Jesus prayed and He prayed a lot. We can and should take that as a sign of just how important prayer is, and I'm thinking that Jesus spent a good amount of time in prayer giving up His own wants and desires in exchange for the Father's. I believe that the more we are able to do that, the better our prayer life will be. We will learn to walk in victory. We will walk through life with an attitude that God is in control. We will gain the victory because we will have let go of the things we hold dear, replacing them with the thing that we come to know that God wants us to hold dear: His will.

More often than not, prayer must be used as one of the greatest weapons the Christian possesses, even if we never come to fully understand it. It is our lifeline to the Father, made possible by the death and resurrection of Jesus, and we are helped by the indwelling of the Holy Spirit.

Chapter 14

Give It Up ...

It is difficult being a fallen human being, isn't it? It does not take much for us to push for our own way and to even corrupt the process of prayer, something God meant for our good.

We often use prayer as if God is our personal genie, and this is most certainly not the case. As we've seen throughout this book, prayer – true prayer – is found not in what God can do for us, but how we can submit ourselves to Him.

There are usually two extremes Christians take part in with respect to prayer. First, we tend to see prayer as something that God wants us to use solely for our own benefit, having our wants supplied as well as our needs. Second, prayer becomes rather rote. It turns into speech without heart. It is very easy to go through the motions of prayer – or even of being a Christian, for that matter – without the heart that God wants us to have and exhibit.

If nothing else, the most important thing we can know and remember about prayer is that prayer is talking *with* God, not at or to Him. In doing so, it becomes a two-way street.

Imagine talking at your spouse or friend without giving them opportunity to interject their thoughts and ideas. It would be a fairly unresponsive and one-sided conversation.

In Isaiah 29:13, we read these haunting words: *"...this people draw near with their words And honor Me with their lip service, But they remove their hearts far from Me, And their reverence for Me consists of tradition learned by rote."*

While God wants to hear from us, He doesn't want us to simply talk *at* or *to* Him. He wants us to talk *with* Him, and we do that by praying His Word and doing so with a desire that is seen in giving up our wants in exchange for His will.

We've seen through this book – and I hope it has merely wetted your appetite as opposed to being the final book you'll ever read on prayer – that it is in the giving up of our will that God becomes Lord and Master of our life.

We've seen examples of how Jesus Himself prayed during the dark times of His life prior to His illegal arrest, trial, and execution. If it is true that Jesus spent time in prayer giving up His own desires, exchanging them for the Father's, how much more should we be doing that? It is obviously extremely important, and it is the beginning of true growth in Christ.

Until we get to this point, we will simply spend our prayer time asking for God to fulfill our wants – the things we perceive as *needs* – when in reality, He has no obligation to fulfill anything except His will for our lives.

Chapter 15

The End

"For all have sinned, and come short of the glory of God." – Romans 3:23

Do you know *when* you will die? Are you aware of the *day* and *hour* when you will slip from this life into eternity? I'm betting you are not privy to that information. So why are you living as if you **_do_** know when it will happen? Putting a decision about Jesus off until another day is taking a huge chance because of the fact that you do not know when you will die. That is plainly simple, and logic alone demands that you do not put this decision off. Yet you do, because the thought of becoming a Christian makes you feel uncomfortable.

You wrongly believe that to become a Christian means that you have to change in a major way *before* Jesus will accept you. It means to you giving up the things you love now because if you love them, then obviously they are wrong and God does not love them.

You are putting the cart before the horse. You must understand that God is not rejecting you. He is not standing there, tapping His foot, demanding that you eliminate those things that He does not like before you can come to Him for salvation.

If you (or anyone) could do that, you would not *need* His salvation at all. It is because you and I do things that are not pleasing to Him that we need His salvation.

What do you do that you would like to no longer do? Do you drink excessively until you cannot control it? Do you play around with drugs? Do you eat too much food until you have become overweight, lethargic and sickly?

What other things are in your life that you do not like? Are you drawn to illicit extra-marital affairs? Do you have a problem with lust? Are you a shopaholic? Do you tend to tell lies a great deal because it makes you feel important, or to hide things about your life?

Do you find that you do not like people and you would prefer to be around animals or out in the woods than around people? Are you a workaholic? Do you place a high value on money and you find that you work very hard to obtain it?

Here's the problem. The enemy of our souls comes to us and tells us that God will never accept us until we get rid of those things. He lies to us that God essentially wants us "perfect" before He will be willing to meet us and grant us eternal life. This is completely untrue.

The other lie that our enemy tells us is that we should not become a Christian because the fun in our life will fly out the door. We will no longer be able to drink or do the fun things we enjoy now. We start to think that coming to God means becoming a doormat for people and having to fill our life with things we do not want to *ever* do.

These are all lies, and unfortunately, too many people believe them. First of all, God does not expect you to be "perfect" before you come to Him for salvation. If that were the case, no one would be able to ever approach Him.

Secondly, God does not say that He is going to take away all the things we enjoy and replace them with things we hate. What is wrong with enjoying the lake on your boat? What is wrong with spending a day with the family fishing or just relaxing in the mountains? There is nothing wrong with these things.

What God *will* do is begin to remove the things that have ensnared you so that life is actually draining from you, but you are not aware of it. For instance, maybe you drink excessively and you have tried everything you can think of to quit. You have gone to AA meetings, spent thousands of dollars on this program or that, and you have even used your own will power to free yourself from the addiction to alcohol, all to no avail.

The question is not: *do I need to quit before I come to Jesus*? The question is: *am I willing to allow Him to work in and through me to take away the addiction I have to alcohol*? Do you see the difference? Are you willing to allow Him to work in you to break that addiction so that you will become a healthier person, one who is able to think straight and one who learns to rely on Him for strength? That is all He wants you to be able to do. He knows you cannot break that addiction (or any addiction for that matter) with your own strength and willpower. Are you willing to allow Him to do it in and through you?

What if you are a workaholic? What if you have "things" like a boat, a house in Cancun, a large bank account, four cars, and more? Do you think that God is going to ask you to give it up, or worse, do you think that God will simply come in and take all of that from you? I know of nothing in Scripture that tells us He will do that.

What God will do with all of those who come to Him trusting Him for salvation is one thing, which begins the moment we receive salvation and will continue until the day we stand before Him. He will begin to create within us the character of Jesus (cf. Ephesians 2:10).

Here is a verse from the Old Testament that was said originally through the prophet Ezekiel to the people of Israel. While this was specifically stated to the Jews, it is applicable to all who receive salvation through Jesus Christ.

"I will give you a new heart and put a new spirit within you; I will take the heart of stone out of your flesh and give you a heart of flesh. I will put My Spirit within you and cause you to walk in My statutes, and you will keep My judgments and do them" (Ezekiel 36:26-27).

God is speaking here through Ezekiel, and He is saying that He will give the people a new heart of flesh, removing that old heart of stone. This is God's responsibility. God is the One who makes that happen. We are told in the book of Hebrews that God is the Author and Finisher of our faith (cf. Hebrews 12:2). This tells me that God is the One who changes me from within so that over time, my desires are slowly turned into His desires.

I recall years ago thinking that God wanted to do everything in my life that I did not want Him to do. I fell into the asinine belief that He wanted to change everything about me. What I learned is that yes, there are things that God does want to change about me. However, there is a lot that God originally gave me that He has also enhanced and used for His glory.

Maybe you are a workaholic who thinks that working hard is something God does not want you to do. This is not necessarily the case.

He may have given you the ability and the knowledge to work in the area of finance for a great purpose. All He may wind up doing is dialing back your workaholic tendencies so that you have more time to enjoy your family and study His Word.

But you say you smoke, or drink, or use illegal drugs, and you don't want to give those up. As I stated, you can't give those up under your own power, and the fact that you have tried so many times has proven it to you.

But God knows what is and what is not good for you. Are you willing to *allow* Him to work in you to change your desires so that you no longer want to smoke, use illegal drugs, or drink nearly as much?

Then you say that you believe God wants to make you a Christian so you can become miserable. Isn't that what most Christians are – miserable? Not the Christians I know, and certainly not me, my wife, or our children.

Where does the Bible say that God wants us miserable? You will not find it. What God wants is for us to be blessed, and that begins when we receive salvation from His hand.

You know, if we would stop and take the time to consider the fact that this life is exceedingly short if we compare it to eternity, we will then realize that there is nothing so important that it should keep us from receiving Jesus as Savior and Lord.

Unfortunately, too many people do not consider the brevity of life. They think they will live forever, or at the very least, they will die when they are really old and gray. That will come too soon. Even though I have just recently turned 54, it still truly seems like yesterday that I was a young boy fishing in the Delaware River near Hobart, New York. There I spent many Saturdays fishing and simply enjoying being outdoors. How did life go by so very quickly? How could that have happened?

It has happened, and I am at a point in life where not only do I realize that this life is short, but I actually look forward to spending eternity with Jesus after this life. Does that sound morbid to you? It shouldn't, because by comparing this life to eternity, we should get a sense of what is truly important.

God does not expect us to become Mother Theresas. He does not necessarily expect us to give up everything and become missionaries in outer Mongolia. What God expects is for us to simply allow Him to change our character as He sees fit.

Over time, we may well find that we have simply stopped swearing without realizing it. Our desire for cigarettes or alcohol has nearly evaporated. Illicit affairs no longer enter the picture.

We also may find that some of the things we want to eliminate in our life become more pronounced. Often the enemy will do this to cause us to focus on something that God is not even doing in our lives at that point. It causes tension, frustration, and self-anger.

If you have gotten to this point in your life and you have not dealt with the question about Jesus, it is about time you do so. You need to stop what you are doing and realize a couple of things before you go through another minute in this life.

- **Sinner**: you need to realize that you are a sinner. You have sinned and you will continue to sin. Sin is breaking the laws that God has set up. We all sin. We have all broken God's laws and that breaks any connection we might have had with God. Sin pushes us away from Him.

    Romans 3:23 says, *"For all have sinned, and come short of the glory of God."* That means you and that means me. All means all. That is the first step. We need to recognize and agree with God that yes, we are sinners. I'm a sinner. You are a sinner. This results in God's anger, what the Bible terms "wrath."

- **God's Wrath**: Romans 1:18 says, *"For the wrath of God is revealed from heaven against all ungodliness and unrighteousness of men, who suppress the truth in unrighteousness."*

This is as much a fact as the truth that we are all sinners. Because we are sinners – by breaking God's law(s) – God has every right to be angry with us and ultimately destroy that which is sinful. If we choose to remain "in" our sinful states throughout this life, we will – unfortunately – be destroyed with the rest of sin.

Fortunately, there *is* a remedy, and it is salvation.

- **God's Gift**: In the sixteenth chapter of Acts, a jailer asks Paul this famous question: *what must I do to be saved?* The question was asked because Paul and Barnabas had been imprisoned, and while there, they began singing praises to God.

God then sent a powerful earthquake that opened the doors to all the prison cells, yet no one escaped. When the jailer arrived, he saw that everyone was still in their cells, and after seeing that miracle (what prisoner would not want to escape from prison?), turned and asked what he must do to be saved. He was speaking of the spiritual aspect of things. He wanted to know how he could be guaranteed eternal life.

The answer Paul gave the man was, *"Believe on the Lord Jesus Christ, and thou shalt be saved, and thy house"* (Acts 16:31).

This is not head knowledge or intellectual assent. This is *believing from the heart*. In fact, Paul makes a very similar statement in another book he wrote, Romans. He says, *"That if thou shalt confess with thy mouth the Lord Jesus, and shalt believe in thine heart that God hath raised him from the dead, thou shalt be saved. For with the heart man believeth unto righteousness; and with the mouth confession is made unto salvation"* (Romans 10:9-10).

When we fully believe something, we confess that it is true. It must begin in the heart because that is where the will is located. We must want to believe. We must endeavor to believe. We must seek to believe.

We must stop giving ourselves all the reasons to deny or ignore Jesus. As God, He became a Man, born of a virgin. He clothed Himself with humanity that He might show us how to live, and in so doing, would keep every portion of the law.

If Jesus was capable of keeping every portion of the law, then He would be found worthy to become a sacrifice for our sin – yours and mine. If He became a sacrifice for our sin, then all that we must do is embrace Him and His sacrificial death.

In short then, to become saved we must:

1. Admit (we sin)
2. Repent (want to turn away from it)
3. Believe (that Jesus is the answer)
4. Embrace (the truth about Jesus)

We **admit** that we are sinner, that we have sinned. This is nothing more than agreeing with God that we have broken His law. Can you honestly say that you have not broken God's law? If you admit to breaking even the "smallest" law, then you are a lawbreaker.

After we admit that we have sinned, the next step is found in **repenting**. Some believe that repenting is actually moving away from sin. This author believes that it is a willingness to move away from sin, and there is a difference.

As we have already discussed, it is impossible to stop sinning. Human beings simply cannot do it because as long as we live, we will have a sin nature, which is something within us that gives us a propensity to sin. As long as we have this inner propensity to sin or break God's laws, we will never be perfect in this life.

We cannot one day say, "Lord, I promise to stop sinning." If we do that, we are only kidding ourselves and setting ourselves up for major failure. We cannot stop sinning in this life. The most we can do is *want* to stop sinning and then spend the rest of our lives allowing God to create the character of Jesus within us, slowly, little by little.

Repenting is to decide that you no longer want to do the things that keep us out of heaven. We no longer wish to break God's laws. It is not promising God that we will never sin again.

Once we admit, then repent, we must **believe**. This is one of the most difficult things to do because believing that Jesus died in our place, that He lived a perfectly sinless life, is extremely difficult to believe. Our minds cannot grasp that truth. We must ask God to open our eyes to that truth so that we can embrace it.

While on the cross next to Jesus, the one thief joined the other thief in ridiculing Jesus. Then, all of a sudden – as we read in Luke 23 – this same thief that had just been ridiculing Him now turned to Him with a new understanding.

It was this new understanding that prompted the thief to say to Jesus, "*Lord, remember me when you come into your Kingdom.*" Jesus looked at the man and responded to him, "*Today, you will be with me in paradise.*"

What had occurred in the mind and heart of that thief from one moment to the next? One thing, and that one thing was that God opened the thief's eyes so that he could see the truth. It was as if the blinders fell off and he now saw and understood who Jesus was, even to the most cursory degree that Jesus was dying not for Himself, but for others.

It was this understanding, this awareness, which prompted the man to ask Jesus to simply be remembered. Jesus went way beyond it to promise the man that he would be with Jesus that day in paradise.

Please notice in Luke 23 that there is nothing in the chapter that tells us that the man promised Jesus he would give up sin, or that he would never sin again. There is nothing that tells us that thief took the time to enter into a final deathbed confession of his sins so that he could be absolved.

The thief made no promises to Jesus at all. What he experienced was the truth of who Jesus was and what Jesus accomplished for humanity. Jesus accomplished what we cannot. What is left is for each person to *admit, repent, believe,* and *embrace*.

Let me clarify here that though we do not see any verbal repentance from the thief, we know that he did repent. He admitted as well. How can we know this? Simply due to the thief's complete about-face with respect to his attitude toward Jesus. One minute, he was ridiculing Jesus, and the next, embracing Him. This is important. There is no way he could have or would have *embraced* Jesus had he not been humbled by the truth *about* Jesus.

Once the thief saw the truth, he was instantly humbled. Within himself, he knew that he was a sinner, and in fact the text states that this is what he told the other thief dying next to him. *"But the other answering rebuked him, saying, Dost not thou fear God, seeing thou art in the same condemnation? And we indeed justly; for we receive the due reward of our deeds: but this man hath done nothing amiss"* (Luke 23:40-41). Something happened within the heart of the one thief. In one moment, the thief went from harassing Jesus to recognizing his own sinfulness, and then ultimately asking for grace, which was freely given to him.

Whether he said it or not, the thief went from haughtiness to humility in a very short space of time, and it was all because he saw the truth about Jesus. That truth helped him realize that he deserved his death and what would happen to him after death. He understood that Jesus did not deserve death.

From here, the thief fully embraced the truth about Jesus and was rewarded with eternal life because of it. He did not come off the cross to be water baptized. He did not list a long litany of offenses against God. He recognized the truth about Jesus, was humbled, and embraced that truth!

This is what each of us needs to do. We cannot give in to the lie that tells us that we are not good enough, or we have not given up enough before God will accept us. We must reject the lie that says we must somehow earn our salvation.

Jesus has done everything that is necessary to make salvation available to us. The only thing that is left for us is to see the truth. Once we see that truth, it should humble us to the point of embracing Jesus and all that He stands for and is to us.

The eighth chapter of Romans begins with the fact that all who trust Jesus for salvation are no longer condemned...*ever*. All of my sins – past, present, and future – have not only been forgiven, but canceled. It is because of my faith in the atonement (death) of Jesus that God is able to cancel all of my sins, even the ones that I have not committed yet. This does not make me eager to commit them. It makes me want to do what I can to avoid sinning.

If you do not know Jesus, please do not put down this book without deliberately *believing* that He is God, that He died for you by the shedding of His blood on the cross, and that He rose three days later because death could not keep Him. Do you believe that? If you do not yet believe it, do you *want* to believe it? If so, then simply ask God to help you come to believe all that Jesus is and all that He has accomplished for you. God will answer your prayers and you may either receive instantaneous awareness of all that Jesus is and has done, or it may be a *growing* awareness over time. In either case, it is the most important decision you will ever make.

Turn to Him now and pray for knowledge of the truth and an ability to embrace it. Please. He is waiting for you.

Ask Yourself:

1. Do you *know* Jesus? Are you in *relationship* with Him? Have you had a spiritual transaction according to John 3?
2. Do you *want* to receive eternal life through the only salvation that is available?
3. Do you believe that Jesus is God the Son, who was born of a virgin, lived a sinless life, died a bloody and gruesome death to pay for your sin, was buried, and rose again on the third day? Do you *believe* this?
4. Do you *want* to *embrace* the truth from #3?
5. Pray that God will open your eyes and provide you with the faith to begin believing the truth about Jesus. Ask Him to help your faith embrace the truth, realizing that you are not good enough to save yourself and that your sin will keep you out of God's Kingdom without His salvation.
6. Pray as if your life depended upon it because *it does*!
7. If you have prayed to receive Jesus as Savior and Lord, please write to me. I want to send you some materials at *no charge or obligation*. Write to me at **fred_deruvo@hotmail.com** and

sign up for our free bimonthly newsletter at
www.studygrowknow.com

Visit our page on **SermonAudio.com/study-grow-know** to hear our latest broadcasts as well as those that have been archived.

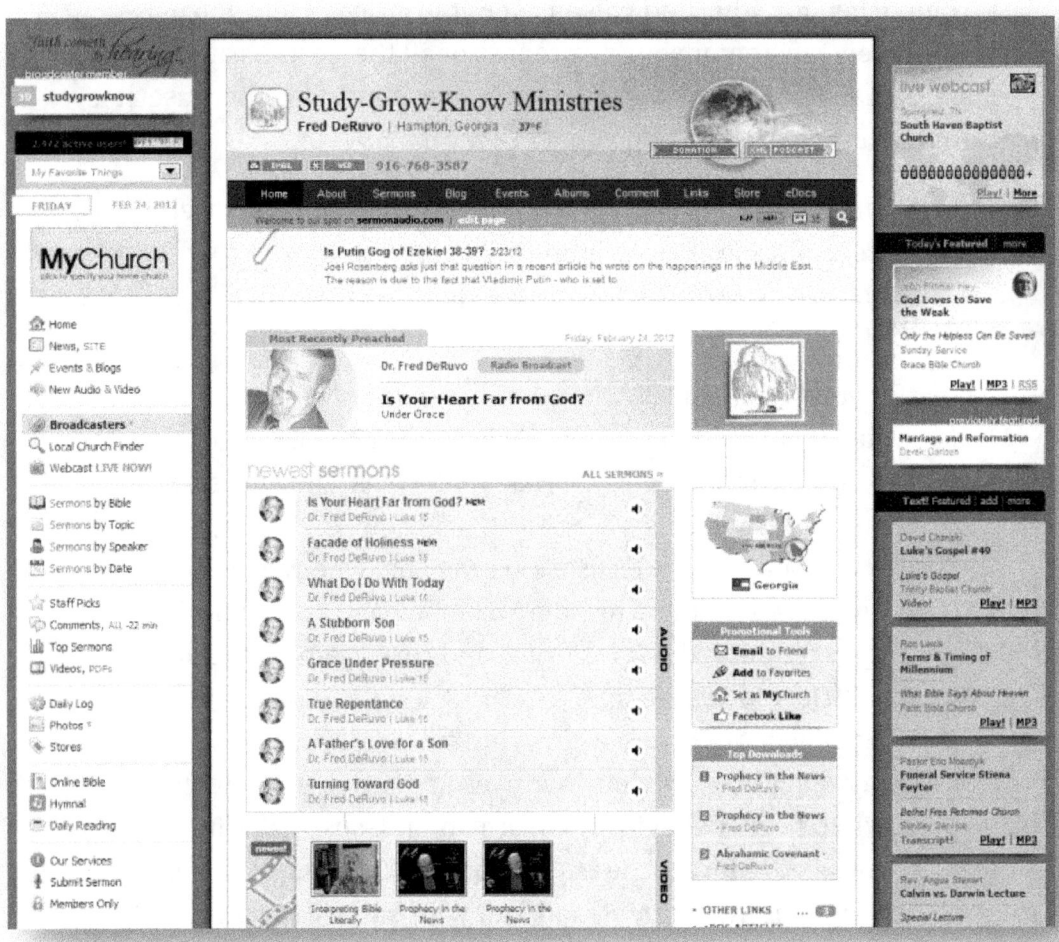

Those who understand the Bible in literal terms are constantly accused of not understanding the Bible in literal terms.

Someone will point to the word "all" or "this" or "that" and charge that the Literalist does not take those words literally, therefore they are not truly understanding the Bible in literal terms.

Is there any truth to this? Does the Literalist strive to understand the literal meaning of the Bible, and by doing so, is he required to understand every word in its most literal sense? ($12.99; 142 pages, ISBN: 978-1441487568)

Christians should always be ready to present the reason for the hope that we have in Christ. However, this is completely different than attempting to win people with arguments and words. What we often fail to remember is that the Holy Spirit is deeply involved in the process of saving souls. We need to rely less on ourselves and more on Him. Either He opens eyes, or He does not.

($11.99; 124 pages, ISBN: 978-0977424467)

Being a Christian is not necessarily a walk in the park. While it begins with the new birth Jesus spoke about with Nicodemus (John 3), this is just the starting point of a lifetime of setting Self's will to the side in favor of fulfilling Christ's will.

($10.99; 100 pages, ISBN: 978-1442110908)

You have to wonder sometimes. Though the visible church is being overrun by Contemplative Prayer, Church Growth movements, Seeker-Sensitive thinking, the Emergent Church, Spiritual Formation and a host of dangerous philosophies that are squelching the authentic gospel with what Paul would call "another" gospel, there are far too many individuals who seem unable to see the forest for the trees. ($13.99; 204 pages, ISBN: 978-0982644317)

Many think they know Dispensationalism and many believe it to be heretical, with some even viewing it as a cult. What is the truth about normative Dispensationalism? This book addresses some of the charges against it in question and short answer format.

($13.99; 194 pages, ISBN: 978-1448632404)

Because of the nature of the times we live in, it is natural to discuss areas of Eschatology (study of End Times). So many events and situations seem to point to the fact that the Tribulation period is right around the corner. During these discussions, all aspects of the End Times are routinely examined, including the timing of the Rapture, the arrival of the Antichrist, the Millennial Reign of Jesus, the coming Gog-Magog (Attempted) Invasion of Israel, and the list goes on. ($13.99; 152 pages, ISBN: 978-0982644386)

A phenomenon is happening today at an alarming rate. More and more people are boldly proclaiming that they are no longer Christians but "ex-Christians." Many are now, in fact, atheists.

Can this be true? If they are non-Christians now, were they truly Christians to begin with? They will state without equivocation that they were in fact committed Christians, but no longer are. What is the deal?

($14.99; 240 pages, ISBN: 978-1442100817)

It should be apparent to every believer that God has one supreme, overarching purpose for everything He does. Every plan He puts in motion, whether directly or by allowing it to occur, is done with that ultimate, singular purpose in mind. The natural question then becomes, what is God's singular highest purpose for everything He has accomplished, is accomplishing, or will accomplish? Is it found in the plan of redemption? ($14.99; 224 pages, ISBN: 978-1442163676)

In progress – coming soon

In progress – coming soon

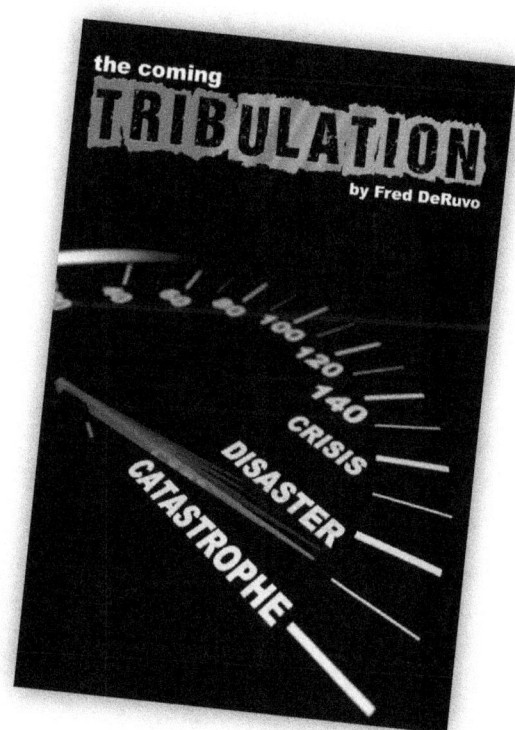

Four verses in the ninth chapter of Daniel are arguably some of the most important verses related to prophecy found anywhere in Scripture. If we are to understand what God has given us in these four verses, then we had better do all that we can to ensure we have a correct interpretation.

The 70 weeks of Daniel, highlighted in Daniel 9:24-27, are there for our benefit. God did not need to tell us anything, but He chose to do so in order that we would be blessed by the information He has graciously provided to Daniel through the angel Gabriel.

($10.99; 77 pages, ISBN: 978-1442189546)

Rather than simply attempting to deal with aspects of this subject which have already been dealt with, author Fred DeRuvo tackles the claims against the PreTrib Rapture from another perspective.

He deals with the plausibility of a few men being able to pull off what has got to be the greatest hoax the church has ever known...if it actually was a hoax. Beyond this, DeRuvo also deals with many other claims by the Anti-PreTrib Rapturist, finding out if these claims hold any water at all.   ($13.99; 168 pages, ISBN: 978-0982644300)

There is huge disagreement about just exactly how Christians are to view their own sin. Some say there needs to be a continual awareness of how bad we are because of our sin and that we need to express absolute remorse to God whenever we commit a sin. If we do not, then God will not take us seriously and sin will not be forgiven.

($11.99; 136 pages, ISBN: 978-0983700647)

What is it that causes people to want to know the secret things of the universe, whether they are true or not? Clearly, knowledge is power, and power can feel absolute when it is kept within a cloistered group.

It appears as though there has been a deliberately hidden, yet clear, goal, known only to those who have been initiated within the various esoteric societies that have existed throughout the ages. These societies use secrecy to draw in those who seek power and dominion over the entire earth through coming cataclysmic changes. ($13.99; 182 pages, ISBN: 978-0983700661)

There is a chaos coming that is predicated upon the rise of Islam, Satanic Soldiers, aliens, and evil beyond measure. As an ideology, Islam masquerades as a religious light to the world, one that promises to usher in world peace – but at what cost? Through the use of political strategies, military might, and religious tenets, adherents of Islam work within various established governments to create special laws or exemptions for Muslims in the hope of eventually overthrowing that established government. Can it happen? IS it happening? Find out in *Evil Rising*. ($13.95; 184 pages, ISBN: 978-0977424429)

We hear all the time how bad things are getting throughout the world. Do we chalk it all up to being the normal cycles that occur in life, or is something else going on behind the scenes? What if this generation alive now turns out to be the last one before Jesus returns? Is there any truth at all to the claim that Jesus will return one day? If you are one who has not taken the time to read through some of the books of the Bible that are said to teach truths regarding the last days, *Living in the Last Generation* puts it out there in a straightforward manner, making it easy to understand. ($11.95; 132 pages, ISBN: 978-0977424405)

ALIENology is somewhat of a science for many who believe that entities from other planets or dimensions enter and leave our dimensions at will. What can we learn from these beings? Anything truthful? Dr. Fred believes that putting our faith in anything these beings say may be a huge leap in the wrong direction. Aliens reportedly come in all shapes, sizes, and even cultural representations. Because of this, there tends to be a good deal of mixed messages out there, yet people believe it because of their experience. Anything wrong with that picture? ($14.99; 176 pages, ISBN: 978-0983700609)

Raised for His Glory delves into the books of Ezekiel and Romans to determine what the Bible actually says about Israel. Is the section on Ezekiel 36-39 speaking of a future time when nations will gather against Israel, or is this something that has already occurred? Moreover, just exactly what is the Valley of the Dry Bones referring to – the nation of Israel, or the Church? Join Dr. Fred as he presents his understanding of these very important sections of God's Word and how they relate to the only nation that He ever created, *Israel*. ($15.99; 190 pages, ISBN: 978-0983700623)

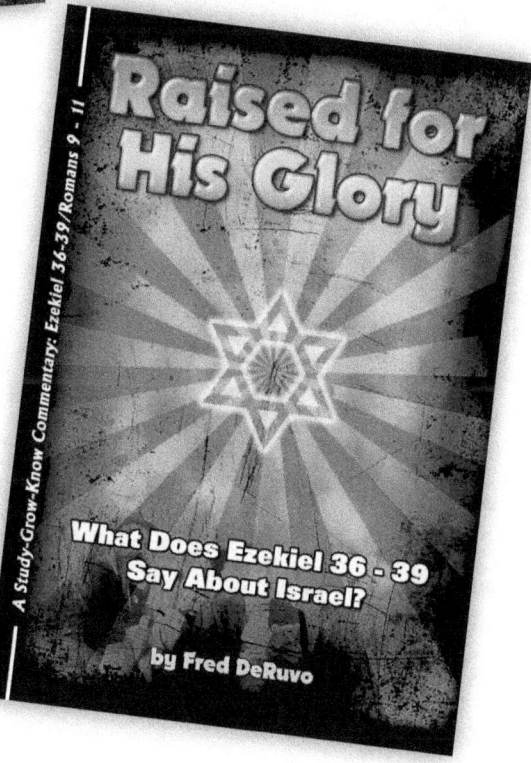

Society has changed drastically over the past decades. Why is that? Simply due to the fact that people have become more preoccupied with *Self*. In this book, Dr. Fred presents *Self* as an entity capable of getting things done its way and using the individual to accomplish it.

In essence, Self easily becomes the master to every person who is not under the control of God's Holy Spirit, with the person becoming the slave. ($14.99; 206 pages, ISBN: 978-0983700630)

In this commentary on Revelation, author Fred DeRuvo draws back the curtain on chapters five through twenty-two, presenting information in an easy-to-understand style, written for the average person. One thing is certain regarding the book of Revelation. Because of its prophetic nature, Christians will continue to debate aspects of it until such a time as we can know for certain. Either the things found within Revelation are yet to come to pass, and that alone will prove their veracity, or they will not come to *pass. Only time will tell.* ($18.00; 392 pages, ISBN: 978-0977424498)

The book of Jude is only twenty-five verses in length, but it packs a spiritual wallop! Jude, the brother of James (and half-brother of our Lord Jesus), writes a message to believers about the times in which they lived. Those times are not at all that much different from the days in which we now live. Jude warns against apostasy, licentiousness, and the mockers that are destined to be part of the last days. Even during Jude's day, mocking the Lord's return had already begun. How much worse is it today, roughly 2,000 years later? ($11.99; 126 pages, ISBN: 978-0983700692)

Everyone has an opinion. It does not matter whether you're a New Ager, a UFO researcher, a student of the Bible, or simply a curious party. Theories regarding aliens range from believing that the whole alien phenomenon is nothing more than an elaborate hoax, to the belief that they are real and getting ready to take over our world, to the view that they are demons disguising themselves as aliens.

($15.99; 206 pages, ISBN: 978-0982644393)

Moo!

ALIENology is somewhat of a science for many who believe that entities from other planets or dimensions enter and leave our dimensions at will. What can we learn from these beings? Anything truthful? Dr. Fred believes that putting our faith in anything these beings say may be a huge leap in the wrong direction. Aliens reportedly come in all shapes, sizes, and even cultural representations. Because of this, there tends to be a good deal of mixed messages out there, yet people believe it because of their experience. Anything wrong with that picture? ($14.99; 176 pages, ISBN: 978-0983700609)

Raised for His Glory delves into the books of Ezekiel and Romans to determine what the Bible actually says about Israel. Is the section on Ezekiel 36-39 speaking of a future time when nations will gather against Israel, or is this something that has already occurred? Moreover, just exactly what is the Valley of the Dry Bones referring to – the nation of Israel, or the Church? Join Dr. Fred as he presents his understanding of these very important sections of God's Word and how they relate to the only nation that He ever created, *Israel*. ($15.99; 190 pages, ISBN: 978-0983700623)

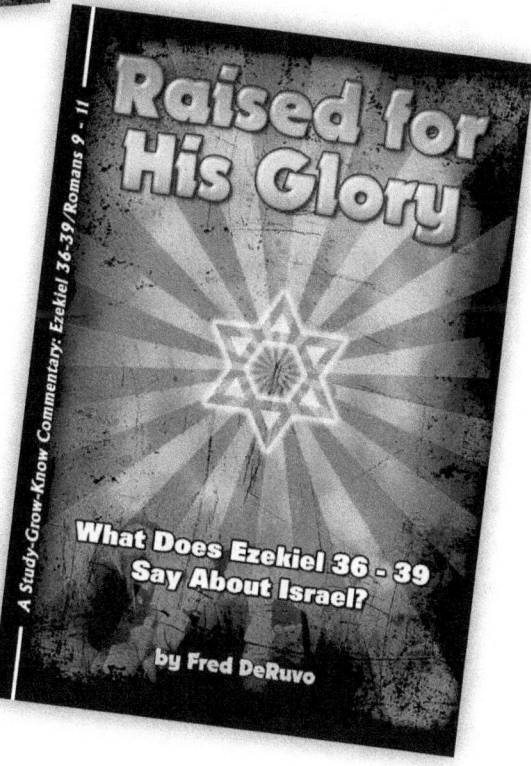

Society has changed drastically over the past decades. Why is that? Simply due to the fact that people have become more preoccupied with *Self*. In this book, Dr. Fred presents *Self* as an entity capable of getting things done its way and using the individual to accomplish it.

In essence, Self easily becomes the master to every person who is not under the control of God's Holy Spirit, with the person becoming the slave. ($14.99; 206 pages, ISBN: 978-0983700630)

In this commentary on Revelation, author Fred DeRuvo draws back the curtain on chapters five through twenty-two, presenting information in an easy-to-understand style, written for the average person. One thing is certain regarding the book of Revelation. Because of its prophetic nature, Christians will continue to debate aspects of it until such a time as we can know for certain. Either the things found within Revelation are yet to come to pass, and that alone will prove their veracity, or they will not come to *pass. Only time will tell.* ($18.00; 392 pages, ISBN: 978-0977424498)

www.ingramcontent.com/pod-product-compliance
Lightning Source LLC
LaVergne TN
LVHW081353060426
835510LV00013B/1809